10 THINGS A HUSBAND NEEDS

FROM

His Wife

ERIN SMALLEY

HARVEST HOUSE PUBLISHERS
EUGENE, OREGON

Cover by Bryce Williamson

Cover Image © Julia_Henze / Shutterstock

Published in association with the Blythe Daniel Agency, Inc., P.O. Box 64197, Colorado Springs, CO 80962-4197, www.theblythedanielagency.com.

10 THINGS A HUSBAND NEEDS FROM HIS WIFE
Copyright © 2017 Erin Smalley
Published by Harvest House Publishers
Eugene, Oregon 97402
www.harvesthousepublishers.com

ISBN 978-0-7369-7046-4 (pbk.)
ISBN 978-0-7369-7047-1 (eBook)

Library of Congress Cataloging-in-Publication Data

Names: Smalley, Erin, author.
Title: 10 things a husband needs from his wife / Erin Smalley.
Other titles: Ten things a husband needs from his wife
Description: Eugene, Oregon : Harvest House Publishers, 2017. | Includes
bibliographical references. | Description based on print version record
and CIP data provided by publisher; resource not viewed.
Identifiers: LCCN 2017011316 (print) | LCCN 2017023192 (ebook) | ISBN
9780736970471 (ebook) | ISBN 9780736970464 (pbk.)
Subjects: LCSH: Christian women—Religious life. | Wives—Religious life. |
Husbands—Psychology. | Man-woman relationships—Religious
aspects—Christianity. | Marriage—Religious aspects—Christianity.
Classification: LCC BV4528.15 (ebook) | LCC BV4528.15 .S63 2017 (print) | DDC
248.8/435 23—dc32
LC record available at https://lccn.loc.gov/2017011316

Printed in the United States of America

17 18 19 20 21 22 23 24 25 / BP-KBD / 10 9 8 7 6 5 4 3 2 1

To my three beautiful daughters:
Taylor, Murphy, and Annie

I love all three of you,
and I'm so thankful to be your mom.

CONTENTS

OPPORTUNITIES AWAIT

W e wives have an enormous opportunity in our marriages. After almost 25 years of marriage, I have decided I want to embrace every opportunity I have with my husband, Greg. I've learned I am the only person who can provide for my husband in ways *no one* else can (and I'm not just talking about sex).

As women, we often assume our husbands get the same kind of affirmation, feedback, and validation from others as we get from our girlfriends. Research shows this just isn't the case.[1] Their friendships and relationships are different. Typically, male relationships center on a shared activity, such as fishing, seeing a movie, or watching a sporting event—not sitting together drinking coffee and affirming one another. The primary source of validation in their lives is us, their wives.

When you begin to meet this void in your husband's life, you will start to realize the level of influence you have in your marriage. You'll be amazed at the changes in your husband's satisfaction and even his disposition as you make the smallest changes. I have embraced the challenge of giving Greg what he longs to hear most from me— affirmation of all the amazing things I notice about him and his behavior. Greg longs to hear me say what he is doing right instead of what he's doing wrong. He needs to hear what I love about him— instead of what I don't.

Recently, in my Bible reading, I came across a familiar story. As I read it, something stuck out to me that I'd never noticed before. In Matthew 27:19, Pilate's wife is distraught about Jesus' impending death—so upset she is even having dreams about Him. She sends word of her dreams to Pilate, begging her husband not to crucify Jesus. As a result, Pilate tries to find a loophole to escape being the one to condemn Jesus to crucifixion.

In numerous readings of this story, Pilate's wife never stood out to me. Looking into her life, I learned she was called "Procula" or "Claudia," and she is noted by scholars for her courage and bravery in approaching her husband during a crisis in his career. Theologians aren't sure how much her message influenced Pilate; however, it may be the reason he washed his hands of Jesus' crucifixion. The question remains, "Was Pilate's response due to his respect and admiration for his wife?" We don't know for sure, but she was a brave woman who had a relationship with her husband that allowed him to receive her message.

If Pilate's wife held sway with her husband's political decisions, what responsibilities and opportunities do I have as a wife? I want to build the kind of relationship where my husband turns to me as a trusted advisor when a huge decision lands on his plate. But what would it take to get him there? I imagine it would require me to be already pursuing him, providing words of affirmation and praise, and listening to him to know what is on his plate in the first place. That's the kind of wife I long to be!

You may be thinking—but what about me? I have needs too! I want my husband to give that to me! Well, of course you do—you're human and a woman! (I get it—I am often the verbal one in the relationship too.) But you can gain a lot of blessings by focusing your energy on being a "giver" instead of a "taker." When we give to our husbands, God will provide for our needs as well. You can never give more than God can give back to you. He is the ultimate giver of life, of gifts, and of every need we have.

Each one must give as he has decided in his heart, not
reluctantly or under compulsion, for God loves a cheerful giver.
2 CORINTHIANS 9:7 ESV

In all things I have shown you that by working hard in this way
we must help the weak and remember the words of the Lord Jesus,
how he himself said, "It is more blessed to give than to receive."
ACTS 20:35 ESV

Whoever knows the right thing to do and
fails to do it, for him it is sin.
JAMES 4:17 ESV

By becoming a model and giving to your husband the things you desire to receive, your husband and your marriage will be shaped in ways you cannot yet imagine.

When you feel loved and cared for by your husband, your heart feels full and complete, doesn't it? Those actions also affect your husband's heart and stir something in him that creates a "cycle" of caring between the two of you.

My girlfriend Kate called me recently and squealed with excitement as she told me what her husband had done upon her return from a recent trip. Randy greeted her in the driveway, dressed up and holding flowers for her. He carried her suitcase into a clean house. He'd cleaned it "spick-and-span" she said. He had prepared lunch for them and then sat and listened to her ramble about her trip for a solid two hours. Dreamy, right?

Now before you start down the road of envy and jealousy and start thinking, "I wish my husband would do that just once!" let me tell you about Kate. She has spent hours talking to me about how to love her husband better. She has prayed endlessly for this man and loved him sacrificially for all five years I have known her. And here she was, her heart overflowing as she shared with me all he had done for her! When we feel loved, our hearts flood open, and as a result, we want to give even more. Although there are no guarantees of his response, your husband will certainly be surprised as you begin to respond differently in your relationship. Whether you show him more affection or appreciation through your actions, affirm him through your words, take notice when he does the things you asked, or join in and enjoy an activity he is interested in, he will receive what he needs most from you. It will not only spur him on, but it will also fulfill your longing for a deeper connection.

Whether your marriage is vibrant or you've "lost that loving feeling," reading this book will help you discover the influence you have in your marriage—to love sacrificially and to meet your husband's needs the way only you can!

Take the challenge to become a wife of influence. Like Pilate's wife, Claudia, you will see how it impacts you and your husband and, most importantly, your marriage. What your husband needs most from you is fully within your possession and your ability—but are you willing to give him this gift?

Faithful heavenly Father,

I come before you and thank you for the gift of marriage! You created marriage and designed it to be a blessing. I thank you specifically for my marriage and my husband. I ask for your power, wisdom, and insight as I begin the journey of reading 10 Things a Husband Needs from His Wife. *I'm not just reading it, but I'm committing to apply it and meet my husband's needs as you lead me. So often I do this in my own strength and will—but this time I want it to be about your leading and guiding me. So, together we can do this! Thank you, Lord, that I can come before you and ask for the Holy Spirit to empower me to the fullest measure. You created my husband to be a priceless treasure—lead me to not just see him as that but to also treat him like a priceless treasure!*

In your precious and holy name, amen.

A HEALTHY WIFE

*Don't just pretend to love others. Really love them. Hate
what is wrong. Hold tightly to what is good.*

ROMANS 12:9 NLT

Chelsea rushed out the door—as she did almost every morning. Her three kids had slammed on the Suburban horn only three times that morning. They weren't the ones who were late—she was. She was late because after making breakfast for all three kids, braiding two dark heads of hair, and making sure lunches were made, she could finally rush into the bathroom to slap some makeup on her aging face and maybe have one indecisive wardrobe change. So each morning, she found herself sprinting into the garage—where her children waited.

After dropping the kids off at three different schools, Chelsea typically sped down the interstate to make it just in time for the daily director's meeting at her high-pressure job. However, today she was rushing to the airport. She had to travel for the next three days, which left more on her plate to make sure each kid had a ride to and from school. Steve helped out when he could, but he had his own set of stressors. He left for work hours before Chelsea and the kids headed out the door, and he arrived home hours after they did. This was life. And at least for the time being, nothing was going to change.

Some mornings Chelsea held her cool, and other days she felt like a crazed maniac in her attempts to get to work on time. Often, she just wanted to make everything stop. To step out of her own life and into someone else's. She wouldn't trade her husband and kids for the world, but still she felt that there wasn't much more of her to go around. She loved Steve, but she knew her marriage was suffering, their relationship taking a back seat to all the other responsibilities on their plates. She needed to make a change, but something always stood in the way. She justified putting off attending to her marriage, believing her husband could always wait (he was an adult) and the kids needed her attention more.

She often heard the women at work talking about their elaborate date nights—exclusive downtown restaurants, morning coffee dates, dinner with other couples—and Chelsea couldn't figure out how they seemed to do it all. "What am I doing wrong?" she wondered. "I can't fit one more thing into my schedule. I'm doing all I can." Then the guilt would surface: "I want to be a great wife—I said my vows on my wedding day—but how can I live up to it all now? I had no idea three kids and a career later, I'd feel so overwhelmed. Somehow, Steve and I manage to stay somewhat connected concerning the kids' schedules and our finances, but we desire more. *I* desire more!"

Maybe you can identify with Chelsea—you are living at a pace you never thought possible, and although you and your husband aren't totally disconnected or even discontent, you desire more. You want to be more intentional about pursuing your husband and building a healthy marriage.

Or maybe your heart longs to be a mom and you've got too much time on your hands. Tension between you and your spouse is on the rise because every time you see the "plus" sign on the ovulation test, you rush to the bedroom to try yet again to conceive the child who will fulfill both your dreams. This adds pressure to your plate and your marriage. You desire to reconnect with your husband on an emotional level—not just around a plus sign.

Maybe you have two small children and you adore your growing family. You are exhausted every evening from wiping noses, changing diapers, and keeping up with the endless piles of laundry. You want more. You desire to nurture your marriage amidst this chaotic season of parenting.

You stay at home, you take the train to work, you work out every morning, you make dinner every night, you mow the lawn, you pour yourself into a nonprofit ministry, you attend MOPS, you attend Bible study, and you even attend Zumba a couple times a week. No matter how different our lives as wives may look, we all have something in common—we desire healthy relationships with one another and a deep connection with our spouse.

You may feel stuck, unsure of how to reconnect with your husband, or you may feel quite pleased with the quality of your marriage—but you must desire something more or you wouldn't be reading this book.

Wherever you are today, I want you to know that I see you and more importantly, God sees you. He sees your desire to encourage the man you married—whether he's young, old, middle aged, retired, or just starting his career. Whatever season you are in, this book is for you. If you desire a deeper connection with your spouse of one year, eight years, fifteen years, or even fifty years, keep reading.

It Starts Here—It Starts with You!

No matter the season you are in, your decision to connect at a deeper level with your husband begins here, and it begins with you.

The simple decision to read this book and to be intentional about discovering what your husband needs most from you is a decision that will forever change your marriage. As you start meeting ten of his most important needs, you may begin to see a change in his behavior as well. Don't be surprised! However, I encourage you to continue on—regardless of his response. Recognize that the journey toward discovering your husband's needs is a choice you are making between you and the Lord. Talk to Him moment by moment and day by day as you pursue the journey to be the wife He is calling you to be.

> A good woman is hard to find,
>   and worth far more than diamonds.
> Her husband trusts her without reserve,
>   and never has reason to regret it.
> Never spiteful, she treats him generously
>   all her life long.
> She shops around for the best yarns and cottons,
>   and enjoys knitting and sewing.
> She's like a trading ship that sails to faraway places
>   and brings back exotic surprises.
> She's up before dawn, preparing breakfast
>   for her family and organizing her day.
> She looks over a field and buys it,
>   then, with money she's put aside, plants a garden.
> First thing in the morning, she dresses for work,
>   rolls up her sleeves, eager to get started.
> She senses the worth of her work,
>   is in no hurry to call it quits for the day
>   (Proverbs 31:10-18 MSG).

Now, we have all heard about this Proverbs 31 woman—over and over again (although you may not have seen this version from The Message). This woman makes many intentional choices about her behavior toward her husband and family as well as the attitude she has toward them and herself. Although I stink at knitting and sewing, there are other things I do to "roll up my sleeves" each day—and all of these choices impact not just me, but my relationships—especially my relationship with my husband.

I am honored you decided to join me on this journey, and I hope you are ready to roll up your sleeves as well. Let's go, girls! Let's look at the first thing your husband needs—it might surprise you!

A Full-of-Life Wife

Here's one thing a husband needs most from his wife, and it may shock you to learn: Your husband desires a wife who is well cared for and full of life. He needs you in more ways than you can imagine. He depends on you for many things and desires you to stick around—not to just be available physically but emotionally as well. Your husband needs a strong, capable "teammate."

> Your husband desires a wife who is well cared for and full of life.

A man can sometimes feel lost without his woman.

My husband and I recently met Bo, a pastor of many years. Greg and I sat with Bo and his second wife, Karen. They have been married for 18 years, and their story is absolutely captivating. Both were widowed more than 20 years ago. After a two-year battle with ovarian cancer, Bo's first wife passed away, leaving him, their three teenage boys, and one little girl, age six, in deep grief. Despite his loss, Bo knew within a few days that he desired to remarry. His first marriage of 25 years had been wonderful, and he wanted to experience that again. He missed the influence of a woman in his life and wanted his young daughter to have a mom in hers.

Karen, on the other hand, lost her husband of 18 years (who was also a pastor) in a tragic hunting accident. She mourned her loss and had no desire to remarry.

When the couple was introduced by a mutual friend, Bo and Karen were up front about where they each stood on marriage from the first phone call. Still they kept talking, and after several phone dates, they decided to meet in person when Karen had a layover in the city where Bo lived.

Bo felt like a teenager as he waited for Karen to deplane. He watched as every single person got off that plane, and still Karen did not show. When the cleanup crew boarded the plane between flights, a flight attendant told Karen she needed to go. As Karen sheepishly walked off the plane, Bo finally saw the blond-haired, blue-eyed beauty he had heard about. They spent the day together enjoying each other's company. A friendship emerged. Within the year, Bo was confident he would marry Karen. After much soul-searching and prayer, and with approval from all four of his children, he asked Karen to become his wife.

By itself, this story is precious and captivating, but I wanted to share it here because strong research indicates a widower will most likely marry within two years. Why is that? Although there are many factors in this equation, I believe it is, at least in part, because men need us ladies! They need the influence of a woman in their life, and apparently, God thinks they do too.

> *It is not good for the man to be alone. I will*
> *make a helper suitable for him.*
> GENESIS 2:18 NIV

However, no woman can give a man everything he desires unless she is well cared for and nurtured. She cannot give from a place of emptiness. Trying to do so just breeds bitterness, exhaustion, and resentment. And women in general have plenty of that. A CDC study found that 16 percent of women aged 18 to 44 reported feeling very tired, exhausted, or otherwise worn out most days, compared with 9 percent of men in the same age range.[1]

I took this to heart last summer. I wanted to be in better shape physically, so I began working out more regularly. A girlfriend asked me if my son Garrison and I would like to climb Pikes Peak with her and her son at some point over the summer. I immediately squealed, "Yes!" This opportunity fit right in line with my goals to care for myself and pump up my workouts. My son enthusiastically agreed to join me on this adventure.

For those who don't know, Pikes Peak is a mountain in Colorado Springs, Colorado. We have lived in Colorado Springs for five years, and frankly I was just tired of staring at its beauty without ever having conquered it. But Pikes Peak isn't just any mountain; it's a 14er—a 14,000-foot mountain! Now, I had heard people tell stories of their climbs up it, and all of them lived through the experience. So I was convinced I could easily do it. It seemed doable, especially since I had increased my workouts.

The day came to set out on our mother/son adventure. We woke up at 3:00 a.m., and we were driving by 3:30 a.m. in order to reach the trailhead by daylight. It was important to reach the summit before the afternoon storms rolled in. After scrambling in the dark to make sure we had all our required gear, we headed up the trail.

Leading up to this, I hadn't asked a lot of questions. For example, "How long is this hike?" "How many hours will it take us?" "How much water do we need to bring?" I did, however, pack tons of Snickers bars in my little backpack.

The trail was steep, and almost immediately my hip flexor began to sting. As we continued our climb, I kept thinking, "Surely, this will flatten out soon!"

It didn't. We continued straight uphill. (Which makes sense, seeing as it's a mountain.) After four and a half hours, we reached the halfway mark. I was nearly out of water already.

My friend pointed out a station with a hand-pumped filter where I could refill from the creek. When I got there, it took me five minutes of continuous strain to pump only about a Dixie cup full of water. So I filled my bottle straight from the creek, without the filter. It was fresh running water—I had always heard fresh mountain water was safe to drink. (Maybe because I was the farthest thing from an outdoor mountain girl.) But it sounded good.

As I gulped my fresh mountain water down, I told my girlfriend what I had done. She gasped, "Beaver fever!"

I looked at her, befuddled. I hadn't learned about *that* fever in nursing school. She explained to me the dangers of parasites that can be picked up when drinking from the same source as wild animals. "Great!" I thought. "Just what I needed!" For the remainder of the hike, I feared I would be featured on the next season of *Monsters Inside Me*.

I had heard that the last mile was the hardest, but three miles out, I hit "the wall." Due to the altitude, the lack of oxygen, and sheer exhaustion (oh, and did I mention dehydration, because I was afraid to drink the beaver fever water?), I was done. But there was no way I was turning back for the nine-and-a-half-mile trip downhill. Up was the only option.

As we continued, our boys were like gazelles up ahead—easily gliding up the trail. I, on the other hand, was like a hippopotamus clomping up the narrow path. Our conversation during those hard miles went something like this: "Do you think this is more difficult than childbirth?" My friend and I nodded our heads simultaneously. "Absolutely. I'd give birth right now if I could get off this mountain." Then, just when I could hardly move any part of my body, I looked up to see my son waiting patiently for his worn-out, exhausted, beaver fever, hippopotamus mother to summit with him. We took the step over the cliff together, and "active labor" came to a screeching halt.

I've never felt so accomplished in my entire life. But those feelings definitely didn't come until someone drove us down the mountain and my oxygen saturation returned to the level of a responsive human being.

Originally, I intended to conquer Pikes Peak to prove I had it in me—to show that my great "self-care" was effective and worthwhile. However, when all was said and done, I'm not sure if I helped myself or harmed myself. My son and I have laughed again and again about our mother/son bonding experience. I never did develop "beaver fever" (although I was certain it was coming many times). As for Greg, he loved hearing about our adventure. He also let me know he had never been so attracted to me as when he heard that I had conquered Pikes Peak. I'm not sure if he found the "beaver fever" story quite as attractive, but it did make him laugh for months to come.

> Take care of yourself with the goal of giving to your husband from a healthy place rather than an exhausted and worn-out place.

I don't know if this activity was ultimately the best way for me to care for myself. There are, however, many other things I consistently do to take care of myself with the goal of giving to my husband from a healthy place rather than an exhausted and worn-out place.

Why Self-Care?

Do you know what it feels like when everyone needs something from you? The baby is crying in the back seat of the car as you race out of the driveway to drop your first grader off at school. Just then you realize you forgot to put shoes on her. You shift the car to park and sprint back into the house. That morning you re-enter the house no less than four times because every time you get to the car, you have forgotten something else.

Finally, you are hot on the trail of the carpool line and your phone rings. It's your next-door neighbor. Your dog is running up the street, and your garage door is wide open. You basically push your child out of the car—as she shoves the last bite of burned bacon in her mouth—so she won't be late. You blow feverish hugs and kisses and speed off right into the rear bumper of another harried mom in front of you in the carpool line. Immediately, you think, "If my husband wasn't out of town all the time, none of this would have happened!" Perfect beginning to the perfect day, right? Does it sound familiar at all?

> Bitterness and resentment come from an empty heart. A wife who is not well cared for cannot care for others.

What I've learned over the years is when I'm exhausted, harried, running on empty, and burning the candle at both ends—no one gets my best. Especially my husband! Usually I can muster up some leftover kindness for the kids, although there are times I flat-out lose it, and when Greg walks in the door at the end of his exhausting day, he barely makes eye contact with me because he knows my glare would set him on fire!

Bitterness and resentment come from an empty heart. A wife who is not well cared for cannot care for others. That is not who I want to be, and I'm guessing you don't want to be that raged, crazed woman either.

Maybe you are more of an internal processor and you don't display your emptiness for all to see. You end up having bitter and resentful internal dialogue. You may not lose it in front of the neighbors, but you have the same chaos playing out within (this gives new meaning to *Monsters Inside Me*).

For years, I lived with guilt knowing I needed to give more to my husband—he was here before we had children, and he'll be here when the kids move out. He deserves my very best and deserves for me to at least make an effort to show him my love. As we care for ourselves, we can then take care of others—especially the men in our lives!

There's a reason a wife's self-care is the primary need out of the ten we'll discuss on this journey. If your husband has a worn-out and weary wife, he isn't going to get those other nine needs fulfilled.

Giving from our emptiness leads to resentment. If he reaches over for you in the middle of the night, you think, "Is he for real? He wants to have sex *now*? Doesn't he get how worn-out I am?" Or if he leaves a sock on the floor or a dish in the sink, you fume, "Really? You can't do your own laundry or clean up after yourself? I work too, you know!"

The list could go on. But this silent fuming is never productive. We don't want bitterness to take root. Hebrews 12:15 says,

Silent fuming is never productive.

"Make sure no one gets left out of God's generosity. Keep a sharp eye out for weeds of bitter discontent. A thistle or two gone to seed can ruin a whole garden in no time" (MSG). As a bit of preventative medicine, then, let's become the best at taking great care of ourselves so *How?* we can also give God's grace to our husbands with a joyful, happy, servant's heart! And we can receive God's grace for ourselves!

For just a few minutes, reflect on how well you care for yourself. Rate yourself zero to ten on how well you are currently doing. Zero, you're running on empty. Ten, you are abundantly full. This isn't a time of judgment—just gentle self-reflection.

It Must Benefit Him

You might be thinking, "This seems rather strange. This is a book about meeting my husband's needs, and I'm being told to care for myself. How selfish!" But I can promise you that taking time and energy to care for yourself will be beneficial to your husband as well. If it's not beneficial to him, then it's not true self-care. Time away with girlfriends or at the gym needs to transpire into more to give to him and others who are important in your life. We are the physical life-givers, and we are also the emotional life-givers...as long as we have something to give.

What, then, does self-care look like?

Jesus told us to love God with all our heart, soul, mind, and strength (Mark 12:30). Let's look at those same four areas through the lens of self-care. This isn't a selfish or narcissistic process—it's just taking care of yourself so you can care for others.

I've filled in four ways you can care for yourself in each area. Fill in the remaining lines with ideas for self-care that are specific to your needs and situation.

Heart

- Listen to your emotions without becoming emotionally driven.

- Become aware of what is going on in your heart and try to put a name to those feelings.

- Value feelings without judging, stuffing, denying them, or letting them dictate your behavior.

- Spend time journaling and expressing your emotion in written form. It's a great way to identify and process emotions.

- *Talk to God when journaling.*
- *Don't let a negative attitude be part of who you are. Be*
- *aware when your mind is negative (ask GOD) → SATAN*
-

Soul

- Sp<u>end time praying.</u>

- Devote yourself to reading Scripture by starting a Bible reading plan. Don't worry if your 90-day plan turns into a 150-day plan. Progress is what matters.

- Commit to a <u>weekly Bible study with</u> like-minded believers.

- <u>Strive to see God in your everyday experiences.</u> (For example, while I'm driving out of my neighborhood, there isn't a day that I'm not praising God as I'm gazing at Pikes Peak.)

- *Pray/worship while driving + walking.*

-

-

-

Mind

- Stimulate your intellect through reading a book for 15 minutes before bed every night.

- Attend classes at a local community college or university on a subject you find intriguing and stimulating.

- Be a lifelong learner—never stop learning! Never adopt the attitude that it's too late to learn new information.

- Take in new concepts and apply them to your life. I absolutely love when a couple comes up to me at a marriage seminar we are leading and says, "We've been married 45 years but have never thought of that in our marriage." We can learn new concepts on any topic—marriage included.

- *Read books — take the time to read instead of watching TV.*

-

-

Strength

- Eat a balanced diet.

- Exercise regularly.

- Establish a regular bedtime that will allow you to get the recommended amount of sleep.

- Schedule regular medical checkups for preventative care.

- Set goals for working out/
  walking/hiking
-
-
-

Now, how are you feeling about self-care? How do you think you are doing now? *GOOD*

How do you think taking great care of yourself will benefit your husband and your family?

A Few Words of Caution from One Woman

Tara and Kent have been married for ten years. In that time they have been on quite a journey—full of good and bad times—but they have persevered with God's help. This is their story.

> *Tara:* I had this preconceived notion of what my marriage would be like. Growing up I had great examples all around me of what a godly marriage looked like, and I expected mine to be exactly like that. I had unreachable expectations from the start of what my husband would do as the leader of our home. I had my husband failing before I even gave him a chance. I was going about the relationship all wrong.

> *Kent:* I had my own preconceived notions, even without realizing it. I felt our marriage should be more like my parents' marriage. But I thought that would happen automatically, and I didn't take the steps to make our marriage meet that standard. I didn't pray the way I should, and I left our marriage open to enemy attacks. I began to give my attention to other things. My job, my hobbies, movies, YouTube, Facebook... They were more important to me than my relationship with my wife, and even more important than my relationship with Christ.

> *Tara:* Around the end of the first year of our marriage, we found out that I could not conceive a child on my own. This heartbreaking news added even more stress to our relationship. Instead of seeking God's help, we just turned inward and pushed each other further away. I felt I wanted more and needed more from my husband. I manipulated him, trying to get him to love me the way my dad loved my mom. I wanted him to act the way I'd

always dreamed of my husband acting. I soon became a people pleaser instead of a God pleaser. I lost my own self-worth and self-esteem because I lost focus of Christ.

Kent: Throughout our marriage I never gave my wife the love and affection that she needed and truly deserved. The kind of love and affection that Christ commands us as men to give to our wives. The longer we were married, the worse I got. I retreated into myself and focused on my wants and desires. I believed the lies of the world about what a marriage looks like (the sitcom marriage). Our communication lines broke down. We started living separate lives. I was blind to what was happening to my wife.

Tara: I had gotten to the point where I felt like we were just roommates and I was his housekeeper. I had no emotional connection with him. I also at that time had just gotten a job that gave me the self-esteem that I had been missing. I was important again, I mattered to someone, I had a reason and purpose again, and people looked to me for my opinion and answers. I made friends who filled the voids Kent didn't. Without recognizing it, I let Satan blind me and use something that was essentially good to turn me against my husband. I let other people—especially other men—fill the gaping hole that was meant for Christ and my husband! I hurt Kent in the worst way: I had an affair. I had built a wall around my heart and let it become hard and calloused toward Kent. I wanted nothing to do with Kent—or with Christ, for that matter.

Kent: Last November Tara had had enough. She told me I needed help, and if I wouldn't get it before the end of the year, she had to leave. Unbeknownst to me, she was already done with me. A few days later we had a huge fight. She walked out the door and didn't come home that night. It was that night that I finally stopped shutting Jesus out of my life. I stopped trying to do it all on my own. I asked God what to do, and He pulled off the blinders I'd placed on myself. When He shone the light, I saw just how far from Him I had strayed. I saw what kind of man I had become, and I wept. I begged God for His forgiveness, and He gave it. But I still felt incomplete, and I now have a better understanding of how two become one flesh. I still felt broken because my wife was not walking with God anymore.

Tara: I had let the ideas and people of this world influence my decisions about moving out and getting a divorce. I had it set in my mind that I had every right to divorce Kent because of all that I had been through. I was living outside of God's will and acting like I was single again. Going out, drinking, and partying with people that weren't Christians. I was planning on divorcing Kent after my parents came to visit for Christmas. I didn't love him anymore. I was just done. But God had different plans.

Kent: That was the hardest time I've ever been through in my life. I was broken and knew that my life and my marriage were beyond what mortal man can fix. I placed my trust in the Lord and began to pray for His healing in our lives and in our marriage.

God's timing is amazing! He brought Tara's parents to us right when she and I needed them the most.

Tara: After my parents came and knocked some sense

into me, I stopped fighting God and my husband. I let them both back in. I opened up to my husband and to Christ and let the healing happen. We started counseling, got more involved in small groups, and surrounded ourselves with friends who were grounded in Christ. It all helped me because Satan had convinced me that I was not worthy of forgiveness and deserved the pain I was going through. The grace and forgiveness I received once I accepted it was amazing! It was a very long, difficult road to where we are now, but now we can use what we have gone through to hopefully help other couples know the power of prayer and the power of trusting in Christ.

Kent: God brought just the right people into our lives in just the right timing. Peers who have been through the same issues, mentors to guide us, marriage counseling when we needed it. We joined a marriage study and really learned a lot about how to go about fighting the Devil instead of each other. The most important thing we now do is read a chapter in the Bible and pray before going to bed, no matter how tired we are. Putting our priorities back where they should be and staying focused on Christ are ways that we make sure we never lose focus again! We have done a sort of cleansing in our lives with the sort of movies, music, and friends we allow to influence our marriage. And because of all of this, we have been given blessing after blessing and are so grateful for the grace and mercy our Lord has given both of us. And we are living examples that in God's power there is always hope for healing.

We can relate to different elements of this story. However, what I don't want you to miss is what Tara attributes to her turning from

God and her husband. She did everything she could to meet his needs with the hope of winning his affection back. But when it didn't work, her heart closed and eventually hardened.

This is a very dangerous place to be individually and in marriage. We become vulnerable to the enemy and to destructive behavior. Satan led Tara right to people who didn't share her morals, values, or faith. She began to be influenced to dishonor her marriage covenant. She ended up in the arms of another man. But praise God for His ability to turn hearts of stone to flesh and to heal and restore hearts and even marriages.

Tara said to me, "It's so shameful that I had an affair—I hate sharing this, but also know that I want God to use our story to help others." She went on to say she wished she could change all of it. But she shared that the benefit of this dark season was the restoration of her soul and her marriage.

I can't stress enough that healthy, balanced self-care is something that benefits all involved—including *you*! Tara was giving at the cost of herself without addressing the deeper heart issues of her motives for serving and meeting her husband's every need. She was giving from a place of emptiness—she was giving from an empty heart. She did it with an agenda that led her to an even more difficult place, at the cost of her integrity and almost the cost of her marriage.

When we take great care of ourselves, we are able to give from our abundance. Therefore, if our husbands don't notice or respond to our efforts, we don't become bitter or desperate. When we know how to care for our own heart, we can give both ourselves and our spouse God's grace. This prevents a bitterness from taking root that will eventually grow into a hardened, dead heart. I cannot emphasize enough the importance of beginning the journey of meeting your husband's needs by being a wife full of life!

CHALLENGE

As you embark on the journey of taking great care of yourself, I encourage you to choose one item from each section you've written above. Commit to doing all four of these things in the next week and then make sure to reflect and note the differences you feel.

Prayer for the Wise Wife

Lord, thank you that you created me to be the more relational being. You made me to care for others. As a wife, Lord, I ask that you help me to be aware of what I can control—me. Help me to make decisions both in my attitude and behavior to show up in my marriage abundantly full and well cared for. You desire me, as your daughter, to live vibrantly—giving your love and all you give me away to others. Thank you, Jesus, for always being there for me and for wisdom and guidance in all aspects of life—but especially in my relationship with my husband. In your precious and holy name, amen!

Prayer for Your Husband

Lord, I lift my husband up to you as I begin this journey. Help him to see how many plates I have spinning in the air. Lord, help him to recognize that I need time away to be refilled and refueled in order to be the best daughter of the Most High King and the best wife to him. Help him to also do the same— to care for himself so he has lots to give, not only to me, but to all those who are in his life. May he care for himself heart, soul, mind, and strength. Lord, bless our marriage relationship as I begin this journey of pursuing his needs. I trust, Lord, that you will meet mine! Amen.

YOUR AFFIRMATION

Kind words are like honey—sweet to the
soul and healthy for the body.

PROVERBS 16:24 NLT

Your husband longs to hear it from no one more than you! His heart longs to hear you say it at the end of a long day. He looks for it and pulls for it through every conversation.

Maybe you are wondering what *it* is.

More than anything in this world, your husband wants to hear you say that he has what it takes. He has what it takes to please you, to be a great father, to be a great provider. He wants to hear that you still find him attractive and that he is worth pursuing. That you see him and notice him.

From a very young age, your husband has had a deep longing in his heart to know that he has what it takes to be successful, to be a man. A real man. John Eldredge put it this way:

> Why do you suppose that when a boy learns to ride his bike with no hands or do his first back flip on a trampoline or hit his first home run, he wants his dad there to see it? And all the crazy things young men do—cliff jumping into rivers, racing motorcycles, all the sports competition—what is fueling all that? Our search for

validation. A man's search for validation is the deepest search in his life. Even if he can't quite put it into words, every man is haunted by the question, "Do I have what it takes?"[1]

Once your husband gave his heart to you, his wife, he desired more than ever to hear it from you. As a new bride and groom, you were both full of anticipation for the shared life ahead. It doesn't always look like you anticipated, but one thing never changes—he longs to be validated and affirmed by you, encouraged after a difficult day at the office, complimented on the job he did putting the kids to bed, and told that you appreciate him more than he could ever know.

Dr. Terri Orbuch spent more than 22 years following 373 couples. By assessing the behaviors of the satisfied, healthy couples in her study, Dr. Orbuch found that one simple thing happy couples do every day is give each other "affective affirmation." She defined affective affirmation as offering "words, gestures, or acts that show your spouse that he or she is noticed, appreciated, respected, loved or desired."[2]

After reading Dr. Orbuch's material, I found the shocking part of her research to be the fact that husbands seem to need affective affirmation *more* than wives. They actually crave it! I went on to learn that this affirmation from wives was found to be the greatest predictor of high marital satisfaction.[3]

Within our female friendships, we women do such a great job affirming one another. We notice the new hairstyle, the new super cute and stylish outfit, or the way we contoured our makeup or decorated our house, dealt with our toddler in the middle of a meltdown, or set a limit with a mouthy teen. We even notice if our girlfriend loses five pounds, and we compliment her. We root for her attempt to complete a marathon or a mission trip. We have the gift of giving words of affirmation to each other. And we freely and frequently offer those words to one another—whether we are best friends, sisters, or complete strangers.

> Men aren't getting the validation their hearts crave. This leaves an amazing opportunity for us wives!

However, our husbands don't typically share in this. When they meet a guy friend for lunch, they don't talk new hairstyles or makeup tips—they talk sports, what they've been doing, and the latest promotion. I was shocked when I realized Greg doesn't really get affirmed in any of his friendships. I just assumed his experience was like mine! After reading this study, I was so surprised, I went straight to Greg, who confirmed it all. The truth is, men aren't getting the validation their hearts crave. This leaves an amazing opportunity for us wives!

Thinking back, I recall Greg often saying things like, "How come you never notice what I do and always are acutely aware of what I don't do?" I always thought it was a creative ploy to get out of trouble with me. But now I realize that all along he wanted affirmation for who he is, not just what he does.

It's not surprising—we all like to hear "job well done," right? But what I really long to hear is that I am worth it; I am valuable, not for what I do, but for who I am.

Recently, I shared this research with a group of girlfriends. They were as shocked as I was. We discussed how we each had seen this play out in our marriages. Each of us could recognize the times we'd missed easy opportunities to affirm our husbands. For example, praising him for being a wonderful daddy after he spent the day with your son at an NBA game, or affirming what a great spiritual influence he is in the home after initiating a time of family devotions, or declaring what a brave man he is to step into a new career field at the age of 50. We all committed to affirming our husbands.

I began to search for at least one way I could affirm Greg every day. I wanted to take advantage of every opportunity to speak life into Greg. I used to think those affirmations, but I guess my pride got in the way of my actually turning those thoughts into words. His response was priceless! He would look at me with a cute, boyish smile. Guess what—I found that pretty attractive (or as he likes to hear—downright *hot*). Not only did my words of affirmation affect him—but they affected how I saw him!

There is a distinct difference between showing gratitude (thanking your husband for what he does) versus affirming him.

Affirmation has two components. The first part is stating a fact—asserting a truth strongly and publicly.[4] So your first job is simply to say what you see in your husband. What character qualities does your husband possess? Is he your protector? Is he bold and compassionate? Dependable, faithful, and forgiving? Is he enthusiastic and discerning? Does he show humility?

The second part of affirmation is offering emotional support or encouragement.[5] You are literally called to speak courage into your husband. Specifically, you can do this by calling out gifts, talents, and character qualities that he may not realize are true about him. Often we can see things in others that they cannot see in themselves.

What about you? Like my girlfriends and me, have you missed opportunities to affirm your husband? In each section below, write down three specific things you appreciate about your husband in that area—and make sure to tell him about what you observe! If you write down character qualities, be sure to also list a situation in which you see those qualities at work. For example, if he's always punctual, write down that you appreciate how he was ready early and had time to help everyone else in the family get ready for church last Sunday. I want to challenge you to give him one affirmation per day for a solid week.

Lover

-

-

-

Friend

-

-

-

Father*

-

-

-

Worker and Provider

-

-

-

---

* If your husband isn't a father, describe situations in which he acts in a fatherly capacity—maybe in a mentorship program, with students, with the children of friends, or with younger members of his own extended family.

Caretaker of Your Home

-
-
-

Life-Giving Words—Like Honey!

Recently I was talking to a couple after a marriage event, and I was honestly a bit taken aback by how the wife was speaking about her husband—right in front of him! He just stood there and quietly took the verbal lashing, his shoulders drooping and his eyes darting for the exit as she spoke.

I finally put my hand on hers and said, "I'm sure you are not aware of how you are coming across, but you're sounding very harsh right now." She looked a little shocked—not that I said something, but because she wasn't aware of how negative she was sounding. I think there are times we are guilty of this.

> *The tongue has the power of life and death, and*
> *those who love it will eat its fruit.*
> PROVERBS 18:21 NIV

The choice comes down to "speaking words of life or words of death" over our husbands—thus reaping the fruit of our words. As we continue to speak words of life over our husbands, we will begin to notice more life-giving behavior and healthy fruit growing in our marriage relationship.

> By encouraging your husband, you are making him courageous.

Remember the second part of the affirmation definition from above? Your job is to offer emotional support and encouragement. Truly, this is speaking words of life. By encouraging your husband, you are making him courageous. Specifically, you can do this by calling out gifts, talents, and character qualities that he may not realize are true about himself.

Calling Out What We See

I remember when Greg started his postdoctoral internship as a psychologist. He had been in graduate school for the first seven years of our marriage, and the day came to finally begin the actual work in the field of psychology. He was so excited after having completed unpaid internship hours for the past four years—he was now ready to begin his first day in the big leagues!

However, after his first full day of seeing difficult clients back to back, he came home absolutely exhausted. He shared that he wasn't sure this was for him, and he said he thought he needed to return to school for something else.

Well, after my initial shock and reaction of "Over my dead body will you go back to school," I was able to meet him with empathy and encouragement. I assured him that I was certain that he blessed each client he had worked with—especially with his witty sense of humor and insightful personality. And honestly, that was all it took...a few words from me, and his confidence was bolstered (it also didn't hurt that I served his favorite meal and his blood sugar began to rise). Often what I affirm in Greg are traits that he simply cannot see in himself.

We have all heard the story of Gideon and the angel of God coming to him as he was hiding in fear from the Midianites. Gideon was from the tribe of Manasseh and was part of an undistinguished family. When his story picks up in Judges 6, he is busy threshing wheat—basically minding his own business. But the angel of the Lord appears to him and says, "The LORD is with you, mighty warrior" (v. 12 NIV). Gideon is dismayed with this and basically tells the angel that he is part of the weakest clan and he is the weakest in his family (v. 15). In essence, the angel of the Lord is able to see what is true about Gideon (that he is a mighty warrior), even though Gideon doesn't see it in the slightest. Gideon ends up defeating the Midianite army despite many disadvantages. He is remembered as a military leader, judge, and prophet.

Just as the angel of the Lord called Gideon a "mighty warrior," we have opportunities every day to "call out" what we see to be true in our husbands. What an opportunity indeed!

Life-Giving Words in Response to Challenges

Women have power in their words in other ways as well. We can offer life-giving words in response to challenges our husbands face. Our job is to be like the operator on the other end of a 911 call. In a desperate situation, her job is to offer life-giving words through her ability to remain calm and give clear direction and hope. Although your husband may not be involved in a life-or-death scenario, he may be very discouraged or down—stressed or feeling lost—and as his wife, you have great influence to be that sound, rational voice in his life.

I was recently reintroduced to a woman in Scripture I really hadn't paid much attention to. I'd overlooked this woman's courage and her impact. We meet Manoah's wife in Judges 13, as she displays great courage in speaking up in response to her husband's fear.

This precious woman is never named in Scripture and happens to be struggling with infertility. However, she has several encounters with an angel of the Lord (while she is by herself) who says to her, "You are barren and childless, but you are going to become pregnant and give birth to a son" (v. 3 NIV). The angel goes on to instruct her to stay away from wine, fermented drink, and anything unclean. Another instruction is that her son's head is never to be touched by a razor, because he is to be a Nazirite, dedicated to God from the womb.

The woman goes to her husband, Manoah, to inform him of this angelic meeting. His response is to pray to God, "Let the man of God you sent to us come again to teach us how to bring up the boy who is to be born" (v. 8 NIV). God hears his prayer, but the angel of God comes again to his wife while she is alone in a field. She runs to her husband, and he runs to meet the angel and converse with him. However, after a conversation and a sacrifice of a goat, the angel ascends to heaven in a flame.

Manoah is sure that they will both be killed because they have seen God. But his wife confidently responds to him, "If the Lord had meant to kill us, he would not have accepted a burnt offering and a grain offering at our hands, or shown us all these things, or now announced to us such things as these" (Judges 13:22-23 ESV).

Manoah's wife not only speaks confident words of encouragement over him as an "emotional life giver," but later she gives birth to the strongest man in Scripture—Samson. She became a physical life giver as well!

How about you and me? Are we willing to speak words of encouragement over our husbands, like the unnamed wife of Manoah? When her husband was ready to give up—knowing that they were surely going to die—she spoke up and offered assurance and encouragement that they would live. I don't know about you, but I want to be like Manoah's wife. When my husband doubts he has what it takes, I want to be confident enough to speak truth.

> When her husband was ready to give up—she spoke up.

Years ago, Greg came home with a long face. He told me his company hadn't met their last quarter budget, and he was concerned about his position. On the inside, I was ready to jump into catastrophe mode: "We'd better call the Realtor and list the house tomorrow!" But instead, I bit my tongue and, with thoughtful intention, tried to reassure my husband. I told him everything would be okay—*we* would be okay—regardless of how budget cuts affected our family.

Seems easy, right? For me, it's more difficult when the emotional stakes are higher. I tend to look only at the bad. But that's not what I want. I want to be that confident voice in my husband's life. I want to be like Manoah's wife.

Can you be the voice of encouragement and reason in your husband's life in the ordinary moments? The times he walks into the house troubled after a difficult day, when his emotions are raw as he wonders if he really has what it takes? Or the times he loses it with your teenage daughter and he feels horrible about it, and you still see all the ways he is a blessing in her life? Can you be the voice of encouragement today?

QUESTIONS FOR REFLECTION

In the past, how have I experienced success in encouraging and affirming my husband? How did he respond?

Where have I gotten stuck? When do I have a difficult time speaking words of life over him?

CHALLENGE

Before you head to bed tonight, I want to encourage you to go to your husband, look him straight in the eyes, and affirm him for something you see in him—a character quality, a strength in his personality, or something you want to call out in him. It would also be a great time to wrap your arms around him and affirm him in words and in deed.

Prayer for the Wise Wife

Lord, I come before you and humbly ask that you make me courageous. Courageous to speak words of encouragement over my husband and to be a confident, encouraging voice in his life. Lord, it's easy to jump on the bandwagon and join in with fear when he is fearful or doubting. Instead, let me turn to you for your strength and confidence. In those moments when I am stuck thinking, "I'm the one who needs encouragement," let me turn toward you, Lord, to get your validation and affirmation. Then when I do receive it—let it overflow from me. Let me speak the words my husband longs to hear—help me tell him I see who he really is, I see how amazing he is, I know he has what it takes, and I see his potential. In your precious and holy name, amen.

Prayer for Your Husband

Lord, thank you for the gift of my husband. Thank you for the man you have made him. Help him to turn to you when he is seeking validation or questioning his worth. In those times when his heart longs for affirmation, may you first and foremost meet that need; however, prompt me, as his wife, to also speak words that are life-giving to him. May he not look to other friends, women, coworkers, or accomplishments to gain affirmation, or look for his value in the wrong place. I give you my husband and ask that you encourage him in Jesus' name. Amen.

VALUE HIS DIFFERENCES

*Be devoted to one another in love. Honor
one another above yourselves.*

ROMANS 12:10 NIV

My husband and I conducted a marriage enrichment conference one Saturday at a church in Fairbanks, Alaska. The night
before the conference, the church hosted a date night event for their
congregation and their community. The evening was set up so that
couples could first go out on a date while the church provided child-
care. The couples then returned to the church for dessert and a short
session led by Greg and me.

Prior to our session, the organizers recreated the *Family Feud*
game. Laughter and fun ensued. Five couples were selected for
teams of men versus women. Questions included: "What would
a man do if he had a day all by himself and his wife was gone?"
The answers were hilarious! They also highlighted the differences
between men and women. The top four answers were *sleep, watch
football, go hunting or fishing,* and *golf.* Several other responses that
shockingly didn't make the top four included *eat, work in the garage,
clean the house.* You can see why several of these wouldn't top the
list for females, right? Some of you may love these activities, but the

hunting and fishing wouldn't be at the top of my list for how I'd want to spend a day alone.

The answer that prompted the most laughter was "have sex!" Of course, upon hearing the roars of his best friends and pastor, the man who gave that answer realized that in this scenario, his wife would be gone all day. Still, it shows sex was on the mind! I was reminded just how different men and women really are.

Men and women are different—and even beyond differences between the sexes, you're different from your husband. Our personalities, likes and dislikes, and our quirks distinguish us from the men we married. That's probably no surprise to you. You might be surprised, though, to hear that our husbands need us to *value* these differences. I hear it time and time again: "We are just so different! It's so frustrating!" But I'm here to tell you that no longer do these differences need to be one of your greatest sources of frustration— they can be something you celebrate and rejoice in. As you know, if the Lord wanted us to be just the same, then He would have made us that way.

He Made Us Different

> *God created human beings in his own image. In*
> *the image of God he created them; male and female*
> *he created them... then God looked over all he*
> *had made, and he saw that it was very good!*
> GENESIS 1:27,31 NLT

God didn't create humanity to have inferior and superior genders. He created them different—as a man and a woman. The following are common "generalizations" about the differences between men and women.

- Men find their identity through their accomplishments; women find their identity through their relationships.

- Men like a clear purpose when communicating: fixing a problem, making a point, or reaching a decision; women focus on relational aspects of communication: processing feelings, discovering common experiences, creating connection, and deepening intimacy.

- Men connect by doing things with others (action-oriented); women connect by talking (relationship-oriented).

- Men want to have sex as a way to emotionally connect with their wives; women want to emotionally connect in order to have sex.

- Men withdraw and want to be alone in their "cave" when under stress; women want to connect and emotionally process when they are stressed.

- Men crave affirmation, appreciation, respect, admiration, doing activities together to feel loved; women desire security, emotional intimacy, and to feel valued, cherished, beautiful, pursued, and captivating to feel loved.

- Men are logical thinkers and can focus on one problem at a time; women are more intuitive thinkers and can multitask.

God notes that all He made was *very* good. I see this reflected when I interact with married couples. I am continually struck by how challenging it is for men and women to figure each other out. I've felt it and heard it from thousands of women: "I'm so frustrated with my husband." Any number of things may lead to this frustration; however, some seem to be universal in marriage. Women will say...

- "He doesn't help around the house."

- "He doesn't show me affection unless he wants to have sex."

- "He won't look at me when I'm talking to him."

- "Whenever I share an issue with him, he always tries to fix it!"

- "He doesn't ever show emotion."

- "When he gets home from work, he goes directly to his chair and doesn't connect with me or the kids."

- "No matter how I try to share why I'm frustrated with him—he takes it personally."

- "If I ask him to do more than one thing at a time, he doesn't seem to be able to do it."

- "He wants to have sex all the time—even after we have had a fight."

- "He often wants to be alone."

- "Sometimes I'll ask him what he is thinking about and he responds by saying 'nothing.'"

Recently, I came across a study that showed the differences in frustrations as noted by males and females. I found it very interesting as to what frustrates men. When asked to rate their top relationship irritants, men and women give strikingly different answers. Here's what grates on us most.[1]

Men's complaints about women:

- the silent treatment
- bringing up things he's done in the distant past
- being too hot or too cold
- being critical
- being stubborn and refusing to give in

Women's complaints about men:

- forgetting important dates, like birthdays or anniversaries
- not working hard at his job
- staring at other women
- being stubborn and refusing to give in

If you have been married longer than a few months, I'm guessing you recognize some of these frustrations. I realize there are different levels of frustration; however, it is common for men and women to feel frustration when they "bump up" against how the other sex engages differently with life on a daily basis. We really are so different.

How Frustration Can Affect Marriage

If we decide to stay in that place of frustration, without acknowledging or understanding what is causing it, we put our hearts and our marriages at risk. In our frustration and lack of understanding, we risk developing bitterness. If we harbor bitterness, our hearts close. A heart that is closed long term eventually hardens.

> If we harbor bitterness, our hearts close.

A hardened heart puts your marriage at the greatest risk. In Matthew 19:8, Jesus replied, "Moses permitted you to divorce your wives because your hearts were hard. But it was not this way from the beginning" (NIV). That is, a hardened heart was never God's design.

Often it is these very differences, quirks, personality traits, and qualities in our spouse that attracted us to him in the first place. When we make our differences the problem, we end up in a tug-of-war, fighting for control in the relationship. We become irritated, negative, disconnected, and in constant conflict, and eventually one or both of us develop a closed heart—and possibly a hardened heart. I want to assure you that differences are truly never the problem or issue. The real issue is how we navigate and manage them.

In order to truly navigate these differences, we must first acknowledge them, understand them, and see them as God-given gifts. Gender differences are only one of many differences we encounter. Others include personality differences, family of origin differences, communication differences, preferences (pet peeves), and habits.

What's the Solution?

We all know what doesn't work—trying to change him! The more I nag, attack, or criticize my husband, the more he will push me away or put distance in the relationship. I can't make him do anything—although I have tried to get creative! (I'm not the only one, right?)

We cannot control our husbands, but we *can* focus on ourselves. We can change our own perspective and how we react to our differences. Remember, God made these differences between women and men and *He* said they were *very* good!

In order to move forward, it is helpful to start recognizing a few small solutions.

> The more I nag, attack, or criticize my husband, the more he will push me away or put distance in the relationship.

- *Accept that we are different.* We must accept that we are truly different. Instead of trying to constantly change each other, we can focus on embracing the truth that the God of this universe knew exactly what He was doing when He made man and woman. I often wonder if He knew that these differences would drive us to our knees, seeking His support, help, peace, and patience!

- *Value the differences.* Instead of despising and becoming sickened at the mere whiff of these differences, we have control over our perspectives, and we can choose to value them! Choose to see the beauty and spice that differences bring to our relationships.

- *Pursue a teammate mentality with our husbands.* We must recognize that we are together in this—allies, not enemies. The enemy (not our husbands, but Satan) would surely love for us to be divided as a result of these differences. It is essential to recognize the power this mentality has over our perspective. When we are teammates, we are one, united, or "for" each other. You see, it is impossible to divide what "God has brought together as one." However, the enemy is sure creative in his attempts to cause disunity in our marriages. Despite our differences, we can remain united when we remind each other that we

are teammates and thus on the same side of the court—
not opposing teams.

- *Understand our differences.* Lastly, seeking to understand
  how we are different is also of essence. We can then
  acknowledge that often we are ticked off over the man-
  nerisms and behaviors that come naturally to our husbands. Many of these differences are actually things God
  gave our spouse to be successful at work or in the roles
  God assigned for him as the protector and provider.

Although all of these solutions are necessary to move forward, I
believe the last one is the most helpful. Ultimately, identifying our
differences will do nothing for us unless we also understand what
makes us different and how those differences affect our relationships.
Only then can we come alongside our husbands and love them well
in everyday ways.

Personality Differences

Gender differences sometimes disguise our personality differences. Much debate surrounds what makes up our personalities,
but without generalizing certain behaviors, talking about personality differences can give us an understanding of general tendencies in
behavior—especially that of our husbands. Opposites attract, and
many of us have married our true opposites. That understanding
alone can bring more grace to how we relate to each other.

Over the past 50 years, studies have led researchers to cite five
dominant personality traits:[2]

- *Extraversion.* How excitable, expressive, and social is
  someone? Those high in extraversion get energy and life
  from being with people. People low in extraversion are

more socially reserved and recharge emotionally by having time alone.

- *Agreeableness.* Regarding overall demeanor, how agreeable is this individual? People high in agreeableness are usually more laidback and cooperative. Those who score low in agreeableness tend to be more competitive and are sometimes seen as manipulative.

- *Conscientiousness.* How does this person typically engage with details and thoughtfulness? Someone high in this area is generally more organized, while someone on the low end may be less goal-oriented and appear more disorganized.

- *Neuroticism.* How stable are this person's moods and emotions? People high in neuroticism may be seen as more moody and irritable, while those low on the spectrum tend to be seen as more emotionally steady and flexible.

- *Openness.* How would you describe this person's creativity, interests, and imagination? Those high in this trait have wide and varied interests, and those low in openness tend to struggle with abstract thinking and lean toward conservative thought.

These broad traits are not meant to explain behavior in totality, nor are they intended to excuse poor behavior or bad habits. Personality traits can be influenced both by our genetics and our environments.

Keep an open mind when looking at these five traits as you try to reach a better understanding of not only your husband but yourself.

A variety of personality tests are available online (Myers-Briggs and the DISC are two examples). If you have never taken one, I encourage you to do so now. Awareness and insight are valuable in any relationship—even Scripture teaches us that!

> *Fools find no pleasure in understanding but*
> *delight in airing their own opinions.*
> PROVERBS 18:2 NIV

One of my favorite prayers is from St. Francis: "O Divine Master, grant that I may not so much seek to be...understood, as to understand."

Instead of getting stuck in our frustrations, wouldn't it be better if we sought to understand our differences—and show our spouses understanding as well? We can begin to gain understanding when we look more deeply at the original common frustrations women experience with men.

The Frustrations We Face

Although you may have personally never experienced these specific frustrations, I would guess you have similar experiences. We can start by asking ourselves where our husbands might be coming from, not to excuse poor behavior, but to allow our hearts to express more grace in navigating our differences.

He Doesn't Help Around the House

Problems like this more than likely arise out of a family-of-origin issue. What roles did his mom and dad take on in the home? Did his father take responsibility for everything outside the home while his mother managed all the household duties? If so, your husband's expectation may be that he will mow the yard and you will take care of everything inside. Are you able to put your frustration aside for a moment, pause, and ask, "Why is he doing this or not doing that?" You could both benefit from a loving, openhearted conversation about each of your intentions and motivations. However, before you have this conversation, I encourage you to spend some time reflecting on your motivations and goals for the conversation. Are you looking to have a more equitable distribution of housework? What specific suggestions do you have that will resolve the issues you're facing?

Over the years, I've let myself become bothered and annoyed by issues that weren't, in the end, all that important. Generally, my negative reactions had more to do with my own heart than with Greg's actions or inactions. I didn't really care about the counters being wiped down; I cared about feeling taken advantage of or disregarded. Once I was able to share the deeper-level feelings, the actual issue seemed less important.

Greg went years without making our bed in the morning. As a matter of fact, he thought it was crazy to make the bed. Still, faithfully, I did it every morning. I had resigned myself to the fact that he didn't value making the bed as much as I did—and that was okay. It was something I desired and decided it was important enough to me, regardless of how Greg felt about it. And honestly, I had no bitterness over this whatsoever. Actually, as I made the bed, I often thought about how blessed I was to have a husband sleeping next to me every night. I looked at it as one task I did for our team.

Until the day came that I had a cast on my leg. I was pathetically flopping my large, heavy new appendage all over the place in order to accomplish the task. Greg walked in on me ferociously struggling to make the bed. I immediately saw it in his eyes that he finally got it. He asked me, "Is this really *this* important to you?"

He knew the answer before I could answer. "Yes," I replied, "It really is." From that day forward, he has made the bed every single day. And when he is out of town, I find myself praying for him and thanking God for my husband while I make the bed.

He Won't Look at Me When I'm Talking

To answer before listening—that is folly and shame.
PROVERBS 18:13 NIV

What women struggle to understand is that men typically do not look at each other when talking either. If your husband's lack of eye contact is at the base of your frustration with him, perhaps knowing that it is simply his nature and not done intentionally can help ease your hurt. Studies have shown that men connect on a deeper lever when shoulder to shoulder with others, whereas women connect eye to eye. For many men, it is not natural or comfortable to sit across from you at a coffee shop to share their deepest feelings from the day. Perhaps face-to-face conversation comes naturally to your husband, but I have found my husband opens up best on a hike or a walk. I still stare at him, but he is free to give me quick glances every now and then. We have learned to navigate this one over many years together.

He Always Tries to Fix Me

Men communicate to achieve something, fix a problem, or give advice. Their goal is to take action. Women communicate to connect relationally, sharing feelings and needs. Their goal is to form a deep connection. As you can see, we have very different goals in our communication and connection styles. I gained a lot of insight the day I realized that when Greg tries to fix something for me, what he is really saying is, "I love you, and I care enough about you to fix the problems." Whether it is offering advice or filling my car with gas, from his perspective, his actions are saying, "I love you and value you enough to spend my time doing this for you." However, as most of us have learned, men are not mind readers. Your husband doesn't have a clue what you truly need unless you tell him.

He Doesn't Show Emotion

Men are more like slow cookers when it comes to reaching the deeper levels of intimacy in communication. It takes time for most men to warm up to a deep emotional experience. We, on the other hand, are more like a microwave oven when communicating emotional content. We can get deep in conversation quickly.

He Doesn't Connect with Me at the End of the Day

When your husband comes home from work, does he head straight for his favorite chair instead of catching up with you or playing with the kids? It's not uncommon behavior. When men are stressed from a long day at work, they tend to isolate and disconnect. This can also be a personality issue if you are married to an introvert. You might try a gentle talk about what you desire—and don't do this when you're steaming mad! Acknowledge that he is made differently and that his body responds differently to stress, but also tell him that you would like to work together to come up with a plan that gives him the time he needs to decompress, but also gives you time to connect at the end of the day.

He Takes Criticism So Personally

Although not exclusively a gender difference, men can be more sensitive to criticism and interpret it as disrespect, while women are more sensitive to feeling unloved or rejected. In chapter 2 we looked at a man's need to know he still has what it takes to be a man, and how he looks to his wife and others for validation. When I address a problem with Greg, he immediately hears, "I'm a failure." Even though I haven't said those words, it's helpful for me to know how my husband perceives what I say. It is important to consider your husband's personality, as more tender and sensitive personalities may be more easily hurt by criticism or negative feedback. Have a conversation with your husband outside a time of high conflict and ask, "When I'm feeling frustrated with you, what are some constructive ways I can express myself to you? I love you, and I want to find a way for us to work through our difficulties together."

He Can Never Manage More Than One Thing at a Time

In general, men do not multitask as well as women because they compartmentalize issues or tasks. It can be helpful for you to encourage him to do one task at a time, and when communicating with him, bring up one topic at a time (rather than every historical issue known to man). This can be difficult, but it ultimately leads to better communication between you and your husband. Greg will get frustrated with me because I can conquer all our issues at once—in my mind! However, if we are talking about Garrison (our 16-year-old son) going to camp for two weeks this summer, it's not a great time to switch to the issues I had today with a lady cutting me off or how someone responded to me at work. A woman's brain allows her to make the leaps between these points of conversation, but a man wants to work on one issue at a time.

He Wants to Have Sex All the Time—Even After We Fight

Did the Lord make us different sexually or what? Men are more easily excited sexually, and sexual intimacy is one of the key ways they feel more connected. After a fight, when he is feeling distance from you, your husband's desire for sex may be his attempt to reestablish a connection. (Remember, he can compartmentalize and keep your fight separate from what happens in the bedroom.) For a woman who connects emotionally and then warms slowly into a desire for sexual intimacy, her husband's on/off switch can be difficult to understand.

He Won't Tell Me What He's Thinking

My life was changed when I found actual research had been done on this pet peeve of mine. I can't recall the number of times I've seen my husband staring into the distance and thought he was lost in deep thought or feeling. I would say, "What are you thinking about?" He would consistently respond, "Nothing." It was a relief to come across this research and realize he hadn't been lying to me all these years.[3] While it can be hard for women to understand, a man's ability to compartmentalize allows him to shut everything down and truly think about nothing. *You* might always be thinking about something, but now you can sleep at night knowing your husband isn't lying to you!

Digging Deep

When our small group meets, it is always wonderful to see couples digging deeper, reflecting on their marriage, and recognizing how they have navigated conflict areas. Couples repeatedly tell us it has been through the successes and failures of navigating their differences that they have learned how to work through problems together. Communicating with each other year after year is the key to understanding what works and what doesn't and to keep *growing* as couples and as individuals. Communication and working together is what makes a great marriage.

From the time we said "I do" 25 years ago, Greg and I have been constantly confronted with our differences. One thing I have learned is that our differences are rarely the problem. I am amazed how much balance Greg brings to me as a woman, wife, and mom. If it weren't for Greg, I would have never learned how to take time to simply relax. He is even-keeled and brings balance to my more emotional style of relating. His sense of humor and perfect timing lighten the mood and bring laughter when I'm getting tense—a real gift when it comes to parenting. Don't get me wrong; there are days I don't appreciate Greg's differences as gifts. Rather than judging him and giving into frustration, though, Greg needs to hear that I value his differences and desire to understand him better.

QUESTIONS FOR REFLECTION

How do differences create conflict in your marriage? Start thinking about how you can identify the differences in your marriage and reflect on how you typically navigate those differences.

Do your differences cause tension in your relationship? If so, how?

How can you seek to understand your husband instead of judging how he is different from you?

I encourage you to use this time to reflect on how your husband's personality is different from yours. How has this brought balance into your marriage?

CHALLENGE

Here's a fun challenge! Take an online personality test with your husband. One of my favorites is the Myers-Briggs. You can actually research how your two personality types interact. For example, I'm an ENFP and Greg is an INFJ, so we would do an Internet search for "ENFP married to INFJ." It will respond with many interesting and fun ways in which your personalities balance each other or could potentially cause friction.

Prayer for the Wise Wife

O Jesus, I come before you as a woman and ask you to help me recognize the differences you made in man and woman. You made us male and female, Lord! Help me to see these differences as very good things, as you deemed them, and to then treat my husband in ways that value him—differences and all. Jesus, if there are issues that need to be worked out, create open hearts to do this. Help me to not be harsh with my words or to choose to stay silent with bitterness brewing. Help me to see my husband as you see him, as a gift. Amen.

Prayer for Your Husband

Jesus, help my husband to recognize that you made him unique. Help him to embrace his God-given strengths as protector, provider, and leader. Help him to see my differences as gifts as well. Help him to keep his heart open to me when I fail and become critical when we bump up against our differences. Bring oneness and unity to our marriage. In Jesus' name, amen.

PHYSICAL INTIMACY AND TOUCH

I have saved many pleasant things for you, my lover.

SONG OF SONGS 7:13 ERV

Every time I write on physical intimacy within marriage, I think, "How much more is there to say about it?" It all comes down to, "Do it often in a way that you both enjoy!"[1]

Wouldn't it be awesome if it was that simple? And it happened that easily? However, with the chaos of life and the fast pace in which we live—work, raising children, running kids to every place under the sun, friends, family, family drama, marriage joys and marriage challenges, and individual issues as well—it seems that many couples are left with the opposite experience in their marriage. They're not doing it often, and therefore, they aren't enjoying it. I have met one too many women who quietly confessed to me, "We haven't had sex in years!" And believe me, I'm not judging you. My heart is breaking for you. Sexual intimacy in marriage is a gift from God.

Each season of life brings challenges and benefits. Maybe you're newly married and still discovering each other. Maybe you have small children and it's hard to find the time and space for intimacy. Maybe you're empty nesters and you struggle to find sex exciting.

Maybe you can't get enough sex, and maybe you feel you would just as soon do without it. Every couple's situation is different.

I encourage you to keep reading and keep striving to connect with your husband passionately. Trust me—it's going to be worth it.

What's Holding You Back?

Do you experience difficulty in connecting sexually with your husband? If so, here are a few possible explanations for that:

    exhaustion
    fear or anxiety
    disconnection
    challenges with orgasm or pain
    menopause or hormonal issues
    distractions, busyness, or lack of priority
    sexual abuse in your past
    recent infidelity in your marriage
    pornography

Exhaustion and Busyness

As women we run at a fast pace, but when we feel worn out, we need to make different choices. I often feel bound by my family's schedule, work, and the kids' activities, but when I really step back to evaluate the situation, there are things I am choosing to do that may not be life-giving or refreshing. Spend some time analyzing how you spend your minutes and see if there are things that can be cut to provide the rest you need.

My husband always encourages me to evaluate what gives me life and what gives me rest. I find the beginning of the school year and the New Year are always great times to evaluate my schedule for balance in these areas. In the Chinese Mandarin language, a symbol for "heart" plus a symbol for "death" equals "busyness." When talking about the impact of exhaustion on our sexual relationship, if you are experiencing "heart death," it makes it difficult to have a great sex life. Sexual intimacy in marriage is more heart related for a woman than anything else. Spend some time evaluating the source of your exhaustion. Is it more emotionally driven or could there be a physical source? Are you low in iron, eating poorly, not sleeping enough? You know the list. Evaluate where this could be coming from. Seek help from your physician if you believe there is a physical cause, or a Christian counselor if you are having a difficult time getting to the bottom of an emotional source.

Fear or Anxiety

At the beginning of our marriage, sex was fun—it was new and exciting. Within thirteen months, I was pregnant. We had a one-month-old on our second wedding anniversary! When number two came along, I developed HELLP syndrome, a pregnancy-related autoimmune disease. My liver shut down and my kidneys began to fail; my body quit producing platelets.

Once they delivered our daughter via emergency C-section, I recovered quickly. I will never forget my six-week postpartum visit. After the doctor completed my exam, he announced I could return to all normal sexual activity. I sat shocked and dismayed, thinking, "What? Why would I do that? It almost killed me last time." And then he told me I should never have another baby. Believe me, that proclamation led to fear in the bedroom. Sex meant babies, and babies meant I could die.

Thank goodness for my faith and a good therapist as I worked my way through these issues. I also turned continually to Scripture to seek God's truth when I felt anxious. God's Word is like a salve to our hearts when we feel anxious or fearful. One of my favorite verses during this time was 2 Corinthians 4:8-9: "We are hard pressed on every side, but not crushed; perplexed, but not in despair; persecuted, but not abandoned; struck down, but not destroyed" (NIV).

We can make choices to draw close to the heart of God—either by studying His Word, listening to praise and worship music, or communing with our heavenly Father in prayer. We need to meet Him face-to-face and connect our hearts with His.

And lo and behold, in faith we had our third child—a son we were told never to have.

Disconnection

Besides fear, emotional disconnection can also affect intimacy in marriage. Think about it—there are seasons of emotional distance caused by increased marital conflict, trust being broken, infidelity, or stress squeezing out through your ears!

A girlfriend, Jenna, shared a story I completely understand.

> We just aren't getting along. We just returned from dropping our first daughter off at college—we fought a lot while we were in Chicago. Abby was irritated with me quite a bit. My husband, Mike, seemed to side with her every time a small altercation broke out. Saying goodbye to her was brutal, and I feel as if I left a piece of my heart in Chicago. But for some reason the tension between Mike and me continued to rise. By the time we arrived home, we weren't really interacting except through sign language. Now, the distance between us feels like the Grand Canyon. At this point we are exchanging only necessary pleasantries. And you know for sure what is out the window—sex! Neither of us have a single bit of desire.

I get it. As a woman and as a wife. I've been through many of the same stages—including launching two daughters to college. The stress levels are high at many different transitions and seasons in the longevity of a marriage relationship.

Challenges with Orgasm or Pain

You may be experiencing one or both of these challenges. If so, there is still hope for a wonderful intimate connection with your husband.

After being married for six months, Becca was certain something wasn't right. She had never experienced an orgasm and wondered what was wrong with her. She began reading online about what she could do and then broached the conversation with a few of her close girlfriends. She learned that there were several things she could try to experience orgasm—although one of the most important was communicating with her husband about it. She did, and together they explored solutions. Ultimately, she discovered that just talking about orgasm and intimacy with her husband drew them to a deeper level of connection.

Now, practically, if you are dealing with challenges with orgasm—know that you are not alone. Although it appears that the actual numbers may vary, several studies indicate that only a quarter of women achieve orgasm during sexual intercourse.[2]

With that said, here are a few suggestions if you are experiencing challenges with orgasm or pain:

- *Talk, talk, talk—with your husband.* It is so important to discuss what you are experiencing with your spouse. Although it may be difficult to bring up initially, like Becca, you will experience a more authentic relationship with your husband. Tell him what you enjoy in bed and what feels good. Ask him to share the same with you.

- *Educate yourself.* Do some research about what you are specifically experiencing. There are many techniques and suggestions that you may find helpful. For example, pelvic floor exercises strengthen your pubococcygeus muscle, which has been found to help with orgasm. Exercise programs have also been found to help in achieving orgasm due to overall improved efficiency of the body.

- *Talk to your doctor.* Definitely seek the help of your physician if things do not improve. They are experts in the human body—including sexuality. Ask questions and seek answers.

- *Relax and keep your mind in the game.* For women it can be difficult to relax when it comes to making love. Our sheer ability to think about 101 things at once can keep us from fully engaging in sex! Give yourself permission to relax and enjoy this time with your husband.

Menopause or Hormonal Issues

There are many different seasons in a woman's life—from PMS to perimenopause and straight into menopause. As our powerful hormones fluctuate, it can impact our outlook on life—can I hear an amen? For me personally, PMS was significant the week before menstruation started. I felt bloated and crampy, and the last thing I could think of was sex! However, I learned to talk to Greg—most of the time I'm certain he already knew what was going on. But I encourage you to not accept hormones or menopause as reasons to stop pursuing a vibrant, intimate sexual relationship with your husband. See your doctor or nurse practitioner to get answers for what works best for you. Options include natural hormone creams or hormones delivered in a variety of methods. Exercise and diet can also impact your overall health when dealing with hormone imbalances. Don't stand idle—seek help and pray, asking God for His help too!

Distractions or Lack of Priority

Women will often share that they didn't recognize the importance of sex in their marriage. Truly, it's easy to get distracted with other things, and suddenly sex moves its way down the list of priorities. Sex doesn't just benefit men. There are also benefits for us women!

- *Decreased stress levels.* Endorphins and oxytocin are released when we have sex. This helps us handle stressful situations. Isn't that ironic—how often have you said, "I can't have sex tonight honey, I am too stressed!" Well, apparently, we need to do just the opposite!

- *Better sleep.* Sex helps to relax your body and mind. When you reach orgasm, prolactin is released—which is also released when we sleep. Although this isn't the answer to all sleepless nights, sex can benefit your sleep and your marriage!

- *Less pain.* It has been found that the endorphins released during an orgasm closely resemble morphine! So, if you have a headache—sex can help ease the pain!

- *Fewer colds.* Sex helps your body release immunoglobulin, which wards off disease, colds, and flu. Do you think you could schedule sex days instead of sick days?

- *A shining glow.* One study found that those who were having sex four times per week actually looked seven to twelve years younger![3] Too bad the cosmetic companies cannot package this. Instead, enjoy sex with your husband!

So clearly, with the benefits to your marriage relationship and the benefits of intimacy for you—it needs to move up on your list of priorities. Plus, sex can be one of the most fun activities you and your husband do together!

Sexual Abuse in Your Past

Oh sweet sisters, if you have endured sexual abuse, I am so sorry! I am guessing that the road to healing has been a long, winding, difficult, and confusing road. Many of my girlfriends have shared their pain with me. One friend, Laura, was abused by her mother's boyfriend as a young girl. Her mom went on to marry the man, sending many confusing messages to Laura. Although her mom didn't know about the abuse, Laura did, and so did her new stepfather. Over the years, God has faithfully provided healing for Laura's heart and soul. Laura said, "Turning to Him with my pain was the best thing I ever did."

If this is your story and you are struggling with intimacy in your marriage, seek help from a licensed Christian counselor, and seek help from the Ultimate Counselor, Jesus Christ. He came that you "may have life, and have it to the full" (John 10:10 NIV). He desires to replace your painful memories with hope and restore what was taken from you. Lean into Him, sweet sister, as you pursue your husband and the gift God designed for you both to experience in a way that brings delight in your marriage! Keep on turning to Him and offering your pain up to Him.

Recent Infidelity in Your Marriage

"I just discovered that my husband has been involved with his assistant. Apparently, this has gone on for months. How am I ever going to trust him again?"

I have had many conversations with women who had just

learned of their husbands' infidelity. These women were devastated. The news of this betrayal is the most difficult you could ever hear. My heart goes out to you, and I am so sorry you are dealing with this in your marriage. But there is hope! I promise you that even in the most difficult scenarios—situations where I humanly couldn't imagine a marriage being restored—I have watched God heal two willing hearts.

For a season, I helped lead marriage intensives that focused on couples who were on their last-ditch efforts to save their marriages. As painful as the stories were, it was equally amazing to see marriages restored. I want to encourage you, sister: If you recently learned your husband has been unfaithful, there is hope! This situation will impact intimacy in your marriage, because sexual intimacy is an emotional, heart-led experience for a woman. Trust must be rebuilt, and over time it can be. The key is two willing hearts coming before the Lord and offering their pain to Him. If you are dealing with unfaithfulness in your marriage, please call 1-800-A-FAMILY and speak to a licensed Christian counselor. Or look into Hope Restored marriage intensives (www.hoperestored.com).

The God of all grace, who called you to his eternal glory in Christ, after you have suffered a little while, will himself restore you and make you strong, firm and steadfast.
1 PETER 5:10 NIV

Pornography

I am sure many of you reading this have been touched or impacted by pornography and lustful impurities in your own homes. If you haven't been, I'm certain you know several couples that have been blindsided by the negative impact of porn or lust. Trust me, the enemy loves that sexual impurity is not just rampant in our world but in our marriages.

I want to assure you that you are not ultimately responsible for your husband's choices around pornography. But porn can invade any marriage, so I am committed to being Greg's teammate in sexual intimacy. Although I am not ultimately responsible for his choices or actions, I can be his greatest ally in battling sexual temptation. Truly, I am the only woman in his life that he can look at sexually, touch sexually, or daydream about without committing a sexual sin. I know that part of my role as his teammate is to help protect him by being available as his lover. This is a massive need that he has from me as his wife, and your husband has from you as well.

If you have recently discovered that your husband is struggling with viewing pornography, you may feel a deep betrayal. It can cause a woman to question her self-worth and her value. If you are experiencing this, you are not alone. It can hit at your core and make you question yourself and also your marriage relationship. The impact is deep, not only for you but also for your husband as it can alter your husband's brain.

In 2014, scientists at Cambridge discovered that the brains of habitual porn users show great similarity to the brains of alcoholics. When a self-confessed porn addict is hooked up to an MRI machine and then shown a pornographic image, a brain structure called the ventral striatum "lights up" in the same way it lights up for an alcoholic who sees a picture of a drink.[4]

Spend some time reflecting on the challenges in your marriage and where they possibly stem from, and identify one step you can take to pursue either emotional or physical healing. No, we are not responsible for a husband's choices or actions; however, we are focusing on what we can control, and that is—you guessed it—*us*!

Again, these roadblocks are not to be taken lightly, but I encourage you to not stand idle, allowing the enemy to rob you and your husband of one of the greatest gifts God has given you in marriage—sexual intimacy.

As you can imagine, any marriage that is left sexless for years will be negatively impacted. Please hear me—I know there is always a bigger story behind why there are problems with sexual intimacy in your marriage, but I encourage you to continue to seek help for whatever issue you're facing. Find a Christian counselor who can help you and your spouse conquer some of these challenges you are facing in your marriage.

I want to stop and pray for you right now. Maybe this area of your marriage is thriving at the moment; know that I am saying the biggest "Amen" and rejoicing for you! However, for some it's challenging—maybe it has only been the past month, or maybe it has been a challenge your entire married life. Either way, it is for all of you I pray:

> Lord, I come before you and ask that you come in close to hear this very intimate prayer. You created marriage—not man. You, God, gave us the gift of sexual intimacy in marriage—not man. Lord, I ask, as these ladies fully enjoy this precious gift, that you would meet them in amazing ways. Sexual intimacy is something that can be so, so good in marriage—and when there are roadblocks in intimacy, it can cause so, so much pain. Jesus, I humbly ask that you meet these ladies as they lay their intimacy challenges before you. Heal them where healing is needed; change their attitudes where an adjustment is needed; and help them to remain open to the gift you have for them and their marriage as a result of pursuing intimacy with you and sexual intimacy with their husband. We ask all of this in Jesus' name! Amen.

We Are Very Different When It Comes to Sex!

Maybe you wonder, "Why does sex mean so much to my husband? Why is it so important to our marriage? Does it really spell connection and intimacy for him?" I'm excited to unpack a few of these issues and leave you with some specific prayers for your man. And yes, this is one of the most important in the list of ten things a husband needs from his wife.

Women Are Like Slow Cookers, Men Are Like Microwave Ovens!

My late father-in-law, Gary Smalley, taught me this concept—women are like slow cookers and men are like microwave ovens when it comes to sex. Typically, men get turned on sexually much faster than women. Women are much slower and much more complex when it comes to our sexual experience. It takes longer to ease into a sexual encounter with our spouse, making us much more like the slow cooker.

This one difference can cause confusion and challenges when it comes to connecting sexually. But again, I am so thankful I can continue to learn and grow.

He Wants Sex and Needs Sex

I love that God made man and woman differently; however, sometimes women think differences are the doom of their marriages. The bottom line when it comes to sexual intimacy in marriage is a man doesn't just desire sex, he *needs* sex. My friend Dr. Juli Slattery discussed this in her book *No More Headaches*:

> Your husband's sexual desire is impacted by what's around him but is determined by biological factors, specifically the presence of testosterone in his body.[5]

There's that word—*testosterone*. It always comes up when there is conversation about a man's sexuality. It drives his sexual development as a teen boy and continues to influence his sex drive over his lifetime. However, it's helpful to understand that he's not just "wanting" sex—his body was created with this need. No, this doesn't mean he can run around like a crazed animal with a wild need for sex—it's just helpful to understand that he is very different from you. Knowing this leads me to a place of compassion for Greg. It gives me a glimpse of how God made him—specifically his physiological need to pursue me, his wife. It is vital that I continue to prepare myself for sexual intimacy as his wife. Since sex is different for me (remember that slow cooker), it's important that I emotionally prepare myself for this experience. I need to make myself ready to receive him. (Think here about the sheer physiology of sexual intercourse—as women we receive our husbands.)

By this I do not want to imply that women do not have sexual needs as well. Although we are created differently, we were created as sexual beings. We discussed the benefits of sex for a woman earlier; however, there is so much more for women to get out of a healthy sex life. God created men with higher levels of testosterone, but women also have testosterone. This hormone helps us to get our sexual engines going too! Sexual intimacy is about serving each other in the bedroom, not just setting your needs aside. Communicate with your husband what you like, what feels good, and what you desire. He doesn't understand what feels good to you—his body is very different. Be assertive and let him know. And always be willing to ask him about what he desires! It makes for a very exciting conversation.

As of late, I've learned that one of the best ways I can prepare myself is to send Greg a flirty text in the morning—letting him know that tonight could be a great night for intimacy. Believe me when I say, he will still be thinking about it when he gets home! As women, it's great to start thinking about it earlier in the day—so we can warm to the experience slowly. My only encouragement is to make sure you are sending the flirty text to your husband before you push send! Awkward if it is sent to anyone else—especially his mother!

Why You Should Make Love Tonight

After 25 years of marriage, our passionate relationship has changed, but I can honestly tell you it gets sweeter with time. Research actually shows that it's normal for passion to decrease after the first few years of marriage.[6] However, simply put, it doesn't take much to start to rebuild it! It is possible to rebuild the passion if both spouses are committed to making small choices to do it.

I have found over the years that the more I understand who Greg is as a man, the more accepting and accommodating I am toward him. Although this information may not be completely earth shattering, I pray that you might come to understand your husband more as you read the rest of this chapter. Imagine we are entering the "sexual education classroom" for understanding your husband.

Sex Can Be a Relationship Reset Button

I've learned when I am feeling distant from Greg, one of the easiest ways to reconnect is to initiate sexual intimacy. Truly, nothing creates a deeper connection between a husband and wife than sex.

Greg has also shared with me that sex impacts how he feels about himself, our marriage, and life in general. Literally, he says it makes him feel that "all is well in the world—and especially in our marriage." In many ways, sex is like life insurance for your marriage.

Sex Can Be Like a Black Friday Shopping Bargain

I don't know about you, but finding a good sale or bargain makes my heart race. I can feel my body flood with endorphins from the excitement! I never know how good the bargain will be, but I'm always striving to find a better deal at the next sale. It leaves me feeling deeply satisfied, happy, and wanting more! I'm guessing you never would have thought about sex being like a sale? But when you think about it—sharing a sexual encounter with your husband can leave you feeling deeply satisfied (most times), emotionally happy, and desiring more excitement for the next time!

Sex Can Be Like a Hot Cup of Tea

After a long, hard day, I love to come into the house and rush up the stairs to grab my favorite comfy pair of pajamas. I'll put the same ones on regardless of the time of day—they are just comfortable and soothing. Then add in a cup of Lady Grey tea and a chair in front of the fireplace, and I'm in my happy place! Sex can be just like that. The tenderness that is expressed between a husband and a wife during sexual intimacy is precious, and it builds a comfort knowing that you are going to continue to know each other in this way for a lifetime. Knowing that I get to make love to this man and be deeply vulnerable with him provides an immense comfort to me. He is the only person in this world that I share that with—and that takes me to my "happy place" in my marriage. As it took time to break in your favorite pajamas, it takes time to become comfortable with your spouse sexually as well. Over the years, it has become sweeter and sweeter.

Sex Can Be Like Christmas Day

In every sexual encounter, there is a gift that you and your spouse get to open up! It's like opening a Christmas present each and every time. You never know for certain what will be waiting. But when all is said and done—I always love what we have "unwrapped." Truly, the excitement that I feel when I open a gift that I have longed for is just the way I feel after intimacy with my best friend (and husband!).

Don't Give Up

The enemy would love to see you hardened toward your husband—especially when it comes to pursuing sexual intimacy. Obviously, he knows the power that intimacy has in marriage. He knows that the Lord gave us the gift of sex in our union; therefore, the enemy hates it. What better way to destroy marriage than to lead couples to stop having sex! He will be the one whispering in your ear, "Your husband doesn't appreciate you, love you, respect you, admire you...(fill in the blank)." He wants to lead you to believe the worst about your husband so you will throw the towel down and say, "Well, then no sex for you!" And of course, Scripture speaks completely again this:

> *Do not deprive each other except perhaps by mutual*
> *consent and for a time, so that you may devote yourselves*
> *to prayer. Then come together again so that Satan will*
> *not tempt you because of your lack of self-control.*
> 1 CORINTHIANS 7:5 NIV

Don't give up. Fight for your marriage! Prepare yourself for sexual intimacy with your husband, recognize that you are very different sexually, and recognize the benefits of intimacy in your marriage.

In order to properly close this chapter on sexuality, we must refer to at least one passage from Song of Songs. As I've studied this passage, it has become a continuous reminder that we do have control over our attitudes and actions when it comes to our sexual relationship with our husbands. I would love to show up like the Shulamite woman in Song of Songs—pursuing her husband, ready to receive him, and promising him pleasant things—both old and new.

I would like your mouth to smell like the best wine. I hope that the wine goes straight to my lover. I hope that it flows gently over his lips and teeth. I belong to my lover, and he desires me. Come, my lover, let us go to the country. Let us spend the night in the villages. Let us go early to the vineyards. We will see if the vine has begun to flower. Perhaps the vines have flowers. We will see if the pomegranate trees have begun to flower. There I will give you my love. You can smell the mandrakes. And you can smell all the special fruits that are near us. Yes, I have saved many pleasant things for you, my lover. There are both old and new things.

SONG OF SONGS 7:9-13 GNT

QUESTIONS FOR REFLECTION

After reading this chapter, what realizations did you have about you and/or your sexual relationship with your husband?

What are your thoughts about being your husband's helpmate and teammate in this area of your marriage? How can you help him with sexual temptations? (Notice I didn't say fix or be responsible for his sexual temptations.)

What is one thing you can do to pursue your husband sexually this week? What is one way you can fight for this area of your marriage?

CHALLENGE

Within the next week, I challenge you to woo your husband sexually. Plan a special night for just the two of you. Since men are visual, wear something sexy and spend extra time getting ready—just like you did when you were dating. Flirt with him throughout the day. And since talking about sex is a huge turn-on for men, ask him some questions. *How could our sex life become even better? What is your favorite place to have sex? What is your favorite position? How often would you like to have sex? What is your favorite turn-on? What is your favorite sexy nightie or lingerie that I wear? What gives you the most sexual pleasure?* At the end of your date, initiate sex. Pull out all the stops. Light some candles, play romantic music, and wear something sexy before you make love.

Prayer for the Wise Wife

Lord Jesus! We come before you and ask that you bless us in our pursuit of healthy sexuality in our marriages. Help us to pursue our husbands both emotionally and physically. Help us to have fun with the gift of intimacy in our marriages. Help us to recognize how we can be the best teammate to battle sexual temptations together with our husbands. Help us to recognize when to speak up and not enable our husbands in temptation or sexual sin and when to show up with empathy. Lord, you created us so vastly different, and this was your perfect will. We ask that you help us always to pursue learning and understanding before we jump into criticism and judgment—especially when it comes to sexuality. Lord, empower us to be in hot pursuit of our husbands! Amen.

Prayer for Your Husband

O Jesus—I come before you and ask that you protect my husband from all sexual temptation and impurity. The enemy loves to taunt and tempt him, knowing that he is easily distracted by sexual images. Jesus, protect him! Lord, may my husband turn to you for help and strength in this battle. May he see that I am his helpmate and teammate and am here for him to assist in this battle. If there is an area where he is struggling, may it come into the light so it can be dealt with. In the darkness the enemy can wreak havoc. I give this all to you, Lord! Amen.

THE BENEFIT OF
THE DOUBT

To the pure, all things are pure.

TITUS 1:15 NIV

Greg recently surprised me when I found him in the kitchen fixing dinner. I really wanted to get a walk in, but I knew the kids would soon begin their nightly "We're hungry" chant.

When I walked into the kitchen, I noticed something smelled rotten. There Greg was, happily chopping his next ingredient for his special concoction, seemingly not concerned with the smell. I checked on the hash browns he planned on using and sure enough, they had been sitting in the fridge for about two weeks instead of frozen. They smelled horrid! But Greg can't smell at all. Not possessing a strong sense of smell might be a good thing on the days when someone in our family has an upset stomach, but when it comes to preparing food for our family, it's not.

I told him the hash browns had gone bad, and as I dug around in the freezer for another package, I could see a look of disappointment engulf his face. Trying to be helpful, I grabbed a few fresh potatoes and shredded them in the food processor. That's when I noticed Greg had chopped an entire onion and put it in the skillet with the rest of the ingredients. I said, "Wow! That's a lot of onion!"

And then he said, "If you want me to ever cook dinner again, you need to stop criticizing how I do it and let me do this my way."

Ouch! I soon recognized that by stepping in and trying to direct dinner prep, I was being inadvertently critical. I realized my "helpfulness" was coming from a place of not being 100 percent sure that Greg could successfully cook a full meal for our family. It came down to my negative beliefs about my husband and my not giving him the benefit of the doubt. I realized if I didn't get myself out of the kitchen and on my walk, it would be a long time before I ever walked into the kitchen to find Greg cooking dinner!

> What we believe about our spouse and how we handle it can have a huge impact on our marriage relationship.

Both what we believe about our spouse and how we handle it can have a huge impact on our marriage relationship.

Are you being invaded with negative beliefs?

Negative thinking can come in many shapes and sizes. It looks different in each scenario, but it tends to show up in similar categories. They are:

{
irrational or false beliefs
unrealistic expectations
illogical conclusions
}

Although our "cover" might look different, these negative beliefs and thoughts show up in the same manner and they have the same impact on our marriages—disaster! When we have negative interpretations or beliefs about our husbands, we begin to find evidence for these in everything they say or do. Have you ever had any thoughts like this?

- "See, he totally thinks I'm the maid—he left his dirty clothes on the floor again."

- "Our account is overdrawn again because he just isn't careful with our finances—he would rather watch Monday night football than figure out our budget."

- "He walked away and didn't even wait for me—he must not care about me like he says he does."

- "He didn't even ask me if I wanted something to drink—but boy, he ordered something. He must only care about himself."

Maybe yours don't look like those, but we all have them—each and every day. They are negative beliefs, and they can wreak havoc in our marriage and other relationships. We look for evidence to prove that our negative perceptions aren't crazy or extreme but reality. There's a fancy psychological term called "confirmation bias," which means we naturally seek to confirm our bias or belief in someone's actions or words.

> Criticism can take its toll on any relationship, but especially on our marriages.

Our husbands have a deep desire to know they have what it takes to be successful. We have such an opportunity to reinforce this through offering them affirmation. One of the number-one complaints of married men is that they feel like they can't do anything right. They report being tired of the nagging and complaining. The bottom line? Criticism can take its toll on any relationship, but especially on our marriages.

Our husbands are asking if they have what it takes at work, at home, and in marriage. If they are met with a continuous stream of criticism, you can imagine that it might lead them to shut down, pull back, "go into the cave," and grow even more insecure about their abilities. Women don't fully comprehend how insecure men are deep at their core. They do everything to cover this up; however, it's there—whether they are young, old, newly employed, or the best in their field. In her book *For Women Only*, Shaunti Feldhahn notes that three-fourths of the men she surveyed admitted to deep insecurity about whether they can cut it and what others think of them.[1]

That's why we have such an opportunity to encourage the men in our lives. Our husbands will tend to live up or down to our expectations of them. No, we aren't responsible for how they feel about themselves, their behavior, or their reactions to us. But while focusing on what we can control—our comments, what we believe about them, and what we ultimately say to them—we can intentionally have a more positive impact on them.

Even in Scripture we are called to this standard. Most of us had this verse recited at some point in our wedding ceremonies.

> *Love is patient, love is kind. It does not envy, it does not boast,*
> *it is not proud. It does not dishonor others, it is not self-seeking,*
> *it is not easily angered, it keeps no record of wrongs. Love*
> *does not delight in evil but rejoices with the truth. It always*
> *protects, always trusts, always hopes, always perseveres.*
> 1 Corinthians 13:4-7 niv

We must fight negative thoughts! When our number-one complaint about our husbands is that they can't do anything right, and the statistics show that our husbands carry around deep insecurities, is there any wonder about the major damage we can inflict when it comes to our negative beliefs?

Prone to Negative Beliefs

As women we are often led by our emotions—sometimes to the extreme of, "If we feel it, it must be true." When Greg and I first married, this was me to the nth degree! However, over the years I have grown in my ability to give him the benefit of the doubt and fight through some of those negative feelings and conclusions.

Women have also been given the gift of a strong intuition, perception, and instinct. This can benefit our marriages in many ways. But when it comes to our husbands, it is best to check our perceptions out. We need to be careful about making snap judgments and assumptions.

Women are stronger than men at reading nonverbal cues. Studies show that women not only better remember the physical appearances of others, but more correctly identify the unspoken messages conveyed in facial expressions, postures, and tones of voice.[2] Coupled with our tendency to "mind read," we tend to default to trusting our emotions and instincts. In doing so, we can end up drawing faulty conclusions.

How Do We Fight This?

One of the most positive things that has impacted how I show up in my relationship with Greg is giving him the benefit of the doubt. This is best described in 1 Corinthians 13:7: "If you love someone, you will be loyal to him no matter what the cost. You will always believe in him, always expect the best of him, and always stand your ground in defending him" (TLB).

As we fight for our marriage relationship, it is important to maintain healthy thinking and beliefs about our spouses. After sharing this concept with a friend who has been married for four months, she shared how she was able to apply positive beliefs in her new marriage almost immediately. She got annoyed with a comment her darling new husband made, and she realized she had a choice in that moment. She could react out of her emotion, which she knew would lead to a bad evening for them both. Or she could remind herself of all her husband does for her and give him the benefit of the doubt that the comment wasn't meant to annoy her. By putting herself in his shoes for a moment and imagining he was tired after a long day, she recognized that her husband wouldn't have intentionally said something to hurt her. She chose to give him the benefit of the doubt and responded with grace and kindness. He then did as well and they ended up having a wonderful night together.

However, in a marriage environment where there is ongoing tension, sometimes it's not the words or deeds that cause trouble. Sometimes conflict is created by the meaning we attach to behavior or words. Often the offending spouse has done little to convey or create that meaning, but once someone attaches a meaning to an event, they likely will accept their interpretation without any need to confirm their belief. Thus, the marriage relationship continues in a downward spiral.

Believe the Best

He really does want to be a great husband. It might be a surprise to you, but your husband likely doesn't lay awake at night thinking about how he can frustrate you all day. He desires more!

My friend Julia shared with me some of the struggles in her marriage. "My husband won't apologize for how he acted. It's been over 24 hours since we spoke. I just don't get why he won't apologize so we can move on!"

After 15 minutes of listening to her and offering validation, I said,

"I know Matt, and he is a good man. I know he wants to be a good husband. And I'm guessing he doesn't have a clue as to what he did or how to make it right."

Within minutes, she packed up her stuff and headed home to see him. She later told me that after arriving home with lunch for Matt, she shared our conversation with him.

"Erin says you want to be a good husband," she told him.

He adamantly agreed.

"Erin says you probably don't know what you did; therefore, you don't know how to make it right." With tears in his eyes, he took her hand and said, "I'm not sure what happened, but I really want to make this right—I'm just not sure what to do."

Although I'm not always that successful with my suggestions (ask any of my girlfriends), this time it worked. I've tried to remind myself in difficult moments in my marriage that the man I married is a really good man, and most of the time when he isn't stepping in to fix the misunderstanding in our relationship, it's because he is struggling to understand what happened. Remembering the truth about who our husbands are in the difficult moments is a powerful, powerful thing to practice.

Fight for Your Relationship

An oft-repeated example of negative beliefs in my marriage occurs anytime I text, call, or say to Greg, "I need to talk to you." Every time he freaks out. My husband thinks these words mean he's in trouble—that what I want to talk about is something he is or is not doing. It could be about the kids, the schedule, me personally, a family member, the weekend plans, or the weather. No matter what mundane issue it is, what he hears is, "You're a failure!"

I have learned not to preface these conversations, but to jump into a casual conversation about whatever topic I think we need to discuss. Sadly, I would guess Greg's negative belief that I need to confront him about his behavior began early on in our marriage when I perhaps did a lot of berating him over one thing or another. It's possible that those early years of our marriage even conditioned him—much like Pavlov's dog—to shut down anytime he hears me say, "We need to talk." If I had it to do all over again, I would have allowed him to make more mistakes, met him with more grace, and set more realistic expectations. This would have led to less "we need to talk" conversations early on in our marriage.

It's one thing to learn how to avoid certain words or phrases we know cause negative thinking in our spouse, but how do we resist rushing to our own negative thoughts about our husbands?

Ask Yourself, "Could I Be Wrong?"

Could you have interpreted your husband's actions or words in an extremely negative way? Perhaps this comes from differences in your perspectives, not from some negative trait in your husband. A humble heart will ask this question knowing that there is a possibility that your thoughts and beliefs are wrong and that wrong thinking is what is leading to your negative feelings and conclusions.

Check the Accuracy of Your Negative Thinking

The next time you begin to reach a negative conclusion, stop to consider alternative explanations for what your husband said or did. Instead of accepting your first negative thought, look for supporting evidence, contradictory evidence, alternative explanations, and more logical conclusions. Encourage yourself to look for evidence contrary to the negative interpretation you usually land at. You can accomplish this either by directly asking your spouse for an explanation, asking clarifying questions, or by making further observations. It may very well lead you to a different conclusion—which is helpful to you and your marriage relationship.

Keep Track of Positive Behavior

Knowing the number-one complaint of married men is they feel they always do the wrong thing, I encourage you to notice what your husband does right instead of what he does wrong. What he is doing instead of what he isn't. On its own, focusing on the positive attributes of your spouse has the potential to increase marital satisfaction. Making this an intentional practice in your day-to-day life can, in the long term, lead to positive beliefs about your spouse's intentions instead of negative ones.

Negative Beliefs in the Bible

Negative thinking isn't a new phenomenon. A great example of this is found in Numbers 12:1-8 (NIV):

> Miriam and Aaron began to talk against Moses because of his Cushite wife, for he had married a Cushite. "Has the LORD spoken only through Moses?" they asked. "Hasn't he also spoken through us?" And the LORD heard this. (Now Moses was a very humble man, more humble than anyone else on the face of the earth.) At once the LORD said to Moses, Aaron and Miriam, "Come out to the tent of meeting, all three of you." So the three of them went out. Then the LORD came down in a pillar of cloud; he stood at the entrance to the tent and summoned Aaron and Miriam. When the two of them stepped forward, he said, "Listen to my words: When there is a prophet among you, I, the LORD, reveal myself to them in visions, I speak to them in dreams. But this is not true of my servant Moses; he is faithful in all my house. With him I speak face to face, clearly and not in riddles; he sees the form of the LORD. Why then were you not afraid to speak against my servant Moses?"

As a result of the Lord's anger, Miriam develops leprous skin for which Moses begs for her healing. The Lord instructs Miriam to be confined outside of the camp for seven days, at which point she could be brought back into the camp. That seems like a severe form of punishment for gossiping and believing negative things about her brother, right?

Don't miss one point in this story. Aaron and Miriam never went to Moses to ask him about marrying a Cushite woman. They simply jumped to a negative conclusion about his relationship and remained ignorant about his motives in doing so. Moses is described to be an "exceedingly righteous person." Moses had a long record of great wisdom and righteousness. Rather than speculate negatively or jump to negative conclusions about his motives, his siblings should have trusted him and given him the benefit of the doubt. Because of their negativity and treatment of Moses, Aaron and Miriam were punished by the Lord for their sin.

As wives, we need to remember who our husbands are and who they are not. Armed with the facts about negative beliefs and understanding our tendencies as women and our need to give others the benefit of the doubt, I encourage you to spend time thinking about your husband's strengths, the things you appreciate about him, and his track record. Keep a list of these qualities handy so you can use them to fight for an accurate perspective of him—especially when you are frustrated and hurt. It's essential!

Don't Avoid Issues

Problems arise in every relationship at some point or another, and the approach taken to resolve those issues will vary. Our nine-year-old daughter, Annie, has a tendency to believe everything is a big deal. When a panic starts to set in, I encourage her to ask, "Is this a big deal or a little deal?" When she slows down and reflects on the big picture, often she will decide that the issue really isn't worth pursuing. This tactic might be useful in your marriage. If something is a "big deal" (i.e. a behavior that is against God's Word, anything that is abusive, or something that is really going to cause you to shut your heart down), then address it with your spouse. However, don't address it in the heat of the moment. Address it with humility and grace. You are much more likely to get that in return. If you decide the issue is not a big deal, then use the techniques on negative thinking and giving others the benefit of the doubt to help you move past this momentary hurt.

God opposes the proud but shows favor to the humble.

1 PETER 5:5 NIV

....
QUESTIONS FOR
REFLECTION
....

Are you infected with negative beliefs, like Miriam and Aaron were? How has this shown up in your marriage?

How have you been with giving your husband the benefit of the doubt? How would your husband respond to that question? How can you battle for an accurate view of him and your marriage?

CHALLENGE

Spend time reflecting on five different scenarios from the past few weeks in which you could have extended the benefit of the doubt to your husband. Think of how that would have practically looked. For example, your husband came home late from work last Wednesday night. You were upset because he didn't call and you needed to be at book club that night. You began to think, "He always does this. He's so inconsiderate." Replay: "I bet he was swamped all day at work and didn't have time to call. He probably rushed home because he wanted to make sure I got to book club as soon as I could." Take it one step further, and watch for opportunities to extend the benefit of the doubt to him over the next week.

Prayer for the Wise Wife

Lord, thank you for my husband. What a gift he is. Help me to become aware of when I'm not seeing him or treating him like that gift. Help me to identify when I'm infected with negative beliefs, and help me to offer him the grace of the benefit of the doubt. Lord, help me to confront any issues that may end up drawing us apart. Keep the enemy away from my mind and beliefs and protect our marriage. In Jesus' precious name, amen.

Prayer for Your Husband

Lord, I thank you for _____. Help him to walk with integrity and be all you are calling him to be. Help him to steer clear of negative beliefs toward me and to share with me when he is feeling like he can do nothing right. Lord, strengthen him in his perception of who you say he is—not the negative messages from me or from the world. Help him to meet me with grace. In Jesus' name, amen.

RESPECT FOR HIS LEADERSHIP ROLE

Respect is like chocolate to a man's soul.

RON DEAL

My friend Macy tells me she learned to respect her husband's leadership the hard way:

> I came into marriage thinking, "I don't need a man. I can do everything myself." Soon, I learned that this wasn't going to get me far in marriage. I decided to really learn what it meant to follow my husband's leadership. I've grown so much in this over our 15 years of marriage. The craziest thing is that instead of bringing up my control issues, it has brought joy, freedom, and also blessing to our marriage.
>
> I've learned that the greatest thing he really needed from me when it came to respecting his leadership was that I trusted him to lead our family. I'm not saying that we don't have discussions about things (we have lots of those), but once we really hear each other out, most times I can truly bless him in whatever endeavor he is pursuing (whether it is buying a car, looking at homes,

or even his ability to judge the character of people). I realized the more I stepped in earlier on, the more I robbed him of the opportunity to learn. What he really needed was the freedom to lead, knowing that he had me excited and cheering him on. He knows when I'm sincerely blessing him with the freedom to lead our family in the direction he feels the Lord is calling us to versus when I'm giving him an insincere, "Fine, just do it!" I love our ability to work together as a team—him as our leader and me as his helper!

I love how committed Macy is to her husband's growth as a leader. Our husbands have been given the position of being spiritual head—as Christ is of the church. But we have differing styles and applications, so this will look different in each of our marriages.

Out of all the topics I've ever written on, the leadership role of a man is one that can drive the most division. The topic has often been misunderstood and misapplied. One of the biggest "shockers" to the women in our small group was when the men shared they felt respected the most when their wives listened to them without correcting or interrupting. Women are often stunned that men tie this to respect. The topic always makes for a lively discussion!

When looking at Scripture, the following verses come to mind...

> *The husband is the head of the wife as Christ is the head of the church, his body, of which he is the Savior.*
> EPHESIANS 5:23 NIV

> *The head of every man is Christ, and the head of a wife is her husband, and the head of Christ is God.*
> 1 CORINTHIANS 11:3 NIV

Following the Leader

In our married small group, we asked the women, "What does it mean to respect your husband as the leader of your family?" The answers were varied:

- Honoring him in my words, actions, and preferences.

- Talking well of him when he is not around.

- Thinking the best of him no matter what.

- Appreciating him—especially in front of the kids.

- Letting him have the final say on matters.

- Allowing him to lead, trusting that he has our relationship in mind.

- Affirming him and validating him.

- Supporting his endeavors.

- Being kind and generous to him.

- Loving him through his decisions.

We asked the men, "What does it mean to be the leader of your family?" They gave a variety of answers as well:

- Loving unconditionally.

- Listening and speaking encouraging words about her around others.

- Being a good husband, father, provider, and protector.

- Relying on God's leadership.

- Total sacrificial love and servant leadership.

- Loving her through difficulties.

- Leading her and the kids spiritually.

Does anything from that list grab you or stand out to you? What does it mean for you to respect your husband as the leader of your home?

Supporting Your Husband

The practical application will be determined between you and the Lord and between you and your husband, but the following ideas will give you a starting point.

Honor Him with Your Words

For me, this means that I honor Greg with my words in front of him and in front of other people. It especially means that I sing his praises in front of the kiddos. They need to hear how amazing their daddy is! Issues that are between the two of us need to remain there. I have only a few friends that I discuss sensitive marriage issues with, and I share only with those who will fight for my marriage with me. I want friends who will support me toward pursuit of my husband—never leading me away. Honoring him in my words, both in his presence and in his absence, is essential.

Honor Him with Your Actions

I believe honoring my husband with my actions begins with my attitude in honoring him. I will never honor him with my actions if I don't value him with my attitude first. My actions will flow out of my attitude. For me, honoring him with my actions includes taking him lunch even when I'm pressed for time, letting him choose where we eat dinner, doing his laundry and putting it away (without complaining), and letting him sleep in—even when I'm tired.

It's the simple things. It won't always be acknowledged—but there is One who will always see you and acknowledge you.

Allow Him to Lead

We will talk more about the *submit* word in the next section, but let's think about what it means to respect your husband's leadership. It was a rude awakening for me when I realized I wasn't actually letting Greg lead. When Greg and I first got married, I had extremely high expectations of what kind of spiritual leader he would be. I remember sitting at the breakfast table, sipping my diet soda (in my pre-coffee days), waiting for him to lead a devotion. Week after week, I was left disappointed. I remember passive-aggressively buying a devotional and leaving it in the center of the table, waiting for him to pick it up and lead me. He was only 23 years old when I married him, and it wasn't until years later that I began to understand the impact my critical and bitter attitude probably had on him. Why would he have had it all figured out? Why would he have wanted to even try to lead if he felt continuously berated? The more I stepped in, the more I robbed him of opportunities to learn how to lead. That cycle wasn't productive in helping him become the leader God called him to be. I'm thankful to say, 25 years later, I'm still learning and so is he! But the difference now is we give each other plenty of room to grow and learn—never expecting perfection.

My friend Sandra shared the same frustration. During an argument one night early in her marriage, her husband, Aaron, confessed he didn't even really know how to lead her. He didn't come from a Christian home and hadn't had a male role model to teach him what that even meant. Sandra realized that her mom had always led because she was a single mom, so Sandra didn't really know how to let him lead either! She soon recognized that she needed to grow as much as he did, and she began to give him the room to do so.

Over the years I've learned that coming after Greg with intensity and emotion concerning his leadership style doesn't go well. I can see it in his face immediately—his face floods and he shuts down. So how can we be supportive and really the "helper" we were designed by God to be?

You Are His Helpmate

> *The LORD God said, "It is not good for the man to be*
> *alone. I will make a helper suitable for him."*
> GENESIS 2:18 NIV

In the garden of Eden everything was perfect. There was no sin, and Adam walked with God. But God saw that Adam was alone.

There is a difference between being alone and feeling lonely. When you are lonely, there is the feeling of isolation and loneliness. Being alone means being without aid or help. Therefore, the Lord created the first human relationship (marriage) to provide help for Adam.

This all makes me smile. I love that the Lord created us as women to be our husband's helpmate—his helper. In God's infinite wisdom, He knew just how to design us to do this job well. He made us with tendencies different from men's. We bring a lot of balance to each other, but those differences can at times bring great frustration too. How can we come alongside our husbands and help them grow into their potential as husbands and as leaders of our homes?

The definition of helpmate is "helpful companion or partner, especially one's husband or wife."

Much like a newly hired CEO has to learn and grow into his role of leadership, our husbands have to grow into their new role. I wish someone had told me this early on. If you are a new bride, or regardless of where you are in your marriage journey, say this out loud:

"_____(name your husband) is learning and growing into the leader of our family. My job, as his helper, isn't to criticize every wrong move, but to help him grow and develop."

It takes trial and error, but I promise you it is worth it. Even if he has been married before, he has never been *your* husband. We used to say to our teenaged daughters, "We have never been the parents of 15-year-old Murphy or Taylor. Can you help us understand you?" I know, it's a different relationship with a husband and a wife, but the point is the same: This man has never been your husband before, and he needs to not only learn how to lead you, but also what his strengths, challenges, and growth areas are as a leader. Give him time and space to grow, and be the best helper you can be!

Praise Instead of Criticism

Don't do what I did—it didn't work! Don't criticize his attempts or take over all together. I've learned over the years there are many styles of leadership and many things I would never have considered to be part of leading. For example, providing financially is part of leading. I would never have thought of that, but when Greg gets up and goes to work every day, he is being a leader. What are the things your husband does that you may not have recognized as leading?

I've also learned that Greg connects to God differently than I do. Gary Thomas explains this well:

> Expecting all Christians to have a certain type of quiet time can wreak havoc in a church or small group. Excited about meaningful (to us) approaches to the Christian life, we sometimes assume that if others do not experience the same thing, something must be wrong with their faith. Please, don't be intimidated by others' expectations. God wants to know the real you, not a caricature of what somebody else wants you to be. He created you

with a certain personality and a certain spiritual temper-
ament. God wants your worship, according to the way
he made you. That may differ somewhat from the worship of the person who brought you to Christ or the person who leads your Bible study or church.[1]

The key for me has been to let Greg be Greg! I was raised in a
very traditional denomination, and, as a result, I connect with God
through more traditional worship. However, Greg connects with
God at his core through being in nature. Once I embraced that there
was nothing wrong with Greg's approach to God (how judgmental
was I?), I was able to let Greg lead me in nature. Now, I love nature
to my core! Living in Colorado has provided us some of the most
amazing experiences, connecting with God in His creation through
prayer or praising Him for His majestic works—the sights we see
every day. We even climbed Pikes Peak together—just the two of
us—and I have never felt more connected to my husband than as
we summited the top of the 14,000-foot peak. Ironically, the best
insight I had for that day was embracing how much easier it was for
me to continue climbing when I was following step-by-step, in sync
with my husband. Following him gave me strength to continue on.

However, toward the end of our five-hour hike, I realized that
it was more effective for me to be in front—and even there I found
comfort knowing Greg was right behind me. There was a safety and a
protection of knowing if I slipped or fell, he would be there to break
the fall. It was a wonderful day of embracing nature, and we walked
away with a real picture of how our relationship works at its best.

I want to encourage you to recognize and embrace the specific
ways your husband leads! He may not be the one to lead a formal
devotional every morning, but I love it when Greg talks to the kids
about God's goodness in the beauty all around us.

Recognize That He's a Work in Progress

Be patient! Let God grow and mature him! Yes, we teach each other a lot in marriage, but let God lead that area too! We are both works in progress; that is how it's supposed to be. Pray for your husband continuously! Pray for godly men to come into his life to help him learn and grow. After a conversation with a male coworker in which he talked about a difficult time he and his family were going through, I realized the best thing I could do would be to introduce him to a male pastor friend. Yes, I basically set them up on a play date. (It was actually a coffee date.) Encourage your husband to spend time with other godly men.

Function as a Team

We have both been given roles straight out of Scripture. Greg has his role as the leader, and I have mine as a helper. Together, we become a beautiful team. Have you ever played on a sports team? In high school I loved playing basketball. All of the girls worked together to attempt winning the game. We supported each other, and we each did our very best at the positions we were assigned. Sometimes that meant stepping up a bit and helping out in another position if it was needed. It didn't really matter who actually scored the points. What mattered was that we worked together to win the game.

The same is true of you and your hubby. You each have your assigned positions—so rock yours and become the best helper you can be. Support your husband's position in your marriage. At times these roles will look different—let's say he is out of town, deployed with the military, or tied up with a busy season at work, and he needs you to step into more of a leadership role. Instead of being bitter, resistant, or refusing to do something that isn't on your list, put your servant hat on and do it. Support your husband's role in his time of need, and together you and he will make a beautiful team.

> *Is there any encouragement from belonging to Christ? Any*
> *comfort from his love? Any fellowship together in the Spirit?*
> *Are your hearts tender and compassionate? Then make me*
> *truly happy by agreeing wholeheartedly with each other,*
> *loving one another, and working together with one mind*
> *and purpose. Don't be selfish; don't try to impress others. Be*
> *humble, thinking of others as better than yourselves. Don't look*
> *out only for your own interests, but take an interest in others,*
> *too. You must have the same attitude that Christ Jesus had.*
> PHILIPPIANS 2:1-5 NLT

The S Word...Submission

I know, I know! We don't like to talk about it. In fact, I believe it is one of the most misunderstood terms and words in our culture. I understand why it is misunderstood and why most women shudder when they hear it. Scripture clearly calls us to submit, but how do we submit if we don't understand what it even means?

> *Wives, submit yourselves to your own husbands as you do*
> *to the Lord...Now as the church submits to Christ, so also*
> *wives should submit to their husbands in everything.*
> EPHESIANS 5:22, 24 NIV

> *This is the way the holy women of the past who put*
> *their hope in God used to adorn themselves. They*
> *submitted themselves to their own husbands.*
> 1 PETER 3:5 NIV

Confusion abounds about what submission means in a practical sense. How do we live it out day to day? Traveling around the country, speaking to couples at marriage events, Greg and I have heard different takes on submission, including, "Let's just ignore it altogether! I don't understand what it is, so I'm just going to act like the word *submission* isn't in the Bible." And that isn't living up to our calling as wives.

What Submission Is Not

- *Blind obedience.* Submission is not about blindly following your husband. I believe God would not have given us fully functioning brains if this was his intent. However, he has given us, as women, the gift of intuition and an ability to reason intellectually.

- *Silence or denying opinions.* This is one that could never work for me personally—or really for you—and for that matter it wouldn't be beneficial to your marriage either. I have many words, and as a strong-willed wife, I cannot be silent. There are times, after I have shared my thoughts, that I will choose to stop talking—but nowhere does it say in Scripture that we are to remain voiceless when it comes to making decisions or respecting our husbands.

- *Abusive.* Unfortunately, submission has at times been used to leave a woman believing she is being called to submit to an abusive husband. NO! NO! NO! This is not the truth! We are daughters of the Most High King! Of course He wouldn't be asking us to be abused at His hand! If your husband is demanding that you submit to anything that does not line up with God's Word, please get help. Go to your pastor, a Christian counselor, or a godly mentor who can share wisdom. If you are in any way being harmed or fearful that you may be in danger, please call a crisis hotline such as the National Domestic Violence hotline—www.hotline.org or 1-800-799-SAFE (7233)—and get to a safe place.

- *Demanded.* Submission is a choice. It is voluntary. It is an action that starts in the heart as a response to our commitment and love of Christ. No husband should demand your submission. Ephesians 5:21 commands us to "submit to one another out of reverence for Christ" (NIV). In essence, husband and wife are submitting to the roles we have been assigned not by man, but by God.

- *Manipulative.* I have heard the most absurd stories of women being manipulated in decisions because they have been led to believe that it is part of submission. Again, in mutual respect for one another and the Lord, there is no manipulation in the submission God has called us to.

Sarah Bessey describes Ephesians 5 in *Jesus Feminist*:

We discover the great paradox hidden within these hotly debated passages of Scripture, tragically misused to subject and berate and hold back, to demand and give place to pride—however benevolent the intention. If wives submit to their husbands as the Church submits to Christ, and if husbands love their wives as Christ loved the Church and gave himself up for her, and if both husbands and wives submit to one another as commanded,

we enter a never-ending, life-giving circle of mutual submission and love.[2]

What Submission Is

First and foremost, let's avoid either extreme. It's incorrect to
say that wives must be submissive because they're too emotional
to make big decisions, but it's equally incorrect to deny that Christ
calls us to submit to our husbands. What, then, is a healthy understanding of submission?

I love how Lisa Bevere breaks it down in her book *Lioness Arising*: "The prefix *sub* means 'under,' and *mission* is an assignment. Put
them together, and we can draw a conclusion that *submission* means
'under the same assignment or mission.'"[3]

The wonderful thing about this definition is that it goes back to
being united, together, and moving in the same direction as one.
It simply means that we are being called together to the same purpose and assignment. Yes, we are respecting our husbands in their
leadership roles; however, our marriages have no power hierarchies
based on race, gender, or social status. In marriage we are equals—
we are simply called to different roles on our team. Think back to
high school basketball...we each have our position. No one is more
important. How do we, as wives, play our role most effectively to
support our team?

> *There is neither Jew nor Gentile, neither slave nor free, nor
> is there male and female, for you are all one in Christ Jesus.*
> GALATIANS 3:28 NIV

Mutual submission comes down to two things—love and respect.
This ties it all together. We started this chapter with looking at our
husband's call to be the leader of our home; then we looked at how

to respect him and support him in this role. Submission ties it all together—love and respect and a spirit of trust between a husband and a wife.

Now some of you may be thinking, "That all sounds great; however, my husband isn't a believer, or my husband isn't reciprocating. What do I do? Am I still called to submit?" Directly out of Scripture we can find that answer:

> *Wives, be subject to your own husbands, so that even if some do not obey the word, they may be won without a word by the conduct of their wives, when they see your respectful and pure conduct...let your adorning be the hidden person of the heart with the imperishable beauty of a gentle and quiet spirit, which in God's sight is very precious.*
>
> 1 PETER 3:1-4 ESV

> Submission ties it all together— love and respect and a spirit of trust between a husband and a wife.

We have an amazing opportunity to hold great influence with our husbands—believing or not! If you are married to an unbeliever, love him wholeheartedly. Be an example of who God is in your life and how He leads you to respect him. The truth is, we can control only ourselves; therefore, pour your heart into the type of wife you are called to be. One that honors, respects, submits, and loves! Pray for your husband, model God's love, and let the Lord do the rest! You will encounter difficult times whether your husband is a believer or not. Turn to your heavenly Father to give you the courage and strength to continue forward.

Simple Ways to Encourage Your Husband

I have compiled a list of simple, everyday ways to love and encourage your husband in his role as the head of your home. I've shared some examples throughout the chapter, but respect, submission, and headship are heavy topics. Here are a few simple suggestions:

- Focus on what your husband does well (Philippians 4:8).

- Speak well of your husband. Don't belittle him to your girlfriends or make him feel unnecessary or incapable (counteract the cultural message that men are buffoons).

- Support him in front of the kids. This includes not dishonoring him in front of the kids—even if you don't 100 percent agree with him. If you need to, step into the other room so you can come to agreement and present a united front in your parenting.

- Notice how he leads your family.

- Don't overwhelm him with words.

- Don't approach him in a harsh, critical manner.

- Give him opportunities to problem solve and fix stuff (ask for advice).

- Give him time to unwind after work—even if you're exhausted too. Even if you are ready to unload about your day at work, the kids' needs, or some crisis, pay attention to your husband's personality. He may need more time to chill after finishing up his work than you usually do. Learn what works best for both of you.

- Brag about him in front of the kids, extended family, and friends.

- Give him opportunity to be physically strong (i.e. open doors, carry heavy things, fix something broken).

- Take an interest in what he's passionate about (i.e. football, fishing, hiking, hobby, etc.).

- Take care of yourself (physically, emotionally, mentally, spiritually).

- Remember that he doesn't multitask like you can—focus on one thing at a time.

- Don't check your phone when you're together (give him your "first fruits").

- Encourage him daily (speak courage into him at the beginning of the day).

- Tell him that you like him—that you want to be with him (be his friend).

- Tell him that you're still attracted to him.

- Don't make him feel stupid or incompetent.

- Realize that men hate sarcasm from their wives.

- Understand how difficult it is to hear criticism—it's like toxic poison to a man's system.

- Stop asking how he feels and ask, "What was the high and low of your day?"

- Live within your financial budget.

- Prioritize fun, laughter, and playfulness.

- Trust his judgment.

- Accept his influence.

- Don't act like his mother (don't mother him).

- Always have his back.

- Ask how you can help.

- Use a gentle tone when confronting him.

- Don't personalize mistakes that he makes.

- Don't correct something that you've asked him to do (i.e. getting your daughter ready for school, loading the dishwasher, cleaning something, etc.).

- Listen without interrupting and let him finish his sentence or thought.

- Be patient when he says that he's thinking about "nothing" or feeling "fine" (don't personalize these statements).

- Don't get frustrated when he can't express or poorly expresses his feelings.

- Don't bring up serious issues when he is tired or hungry.

- Don't expect him to be able to communicate at a deep, emotional level as fast as you can.

- Don't launch into conversation without asking if it is a good time (don't "draft" him into a conversation).

- Pray for him.

- Don't put him on the spot.

- Develop your own spiritual relationship with God.

- Greet him with enthusiasm when he comes home (act like you're glad to see him).

- Don't openly or aggressively challenge his thinking or decisions in front of others.

- Extend God's grace to him and be forgiving when he offends you.

- Ask him to complete this statement, "I feel loved when you..."

The wife must respect her husband.
EPHESIANS 5:33 NIV

QUESTIONS FOR REFLECTION

After reading this chapter, how have your thoughts changed about respecting your husband as the leader of your home?

Do you have a difficult time (like I did) allowing your husband to lead you? What are two things you could do to support him?

Do you relate to the concept of submission being misapplied and confusing? What are your thoughts now about what submission really means?

Out of the list of simple ways to encourage your husband as the leader of your home, which ones do you want to apply? Why?

CHALLENGE

Refer to the list "Simple Ways to Encourage Your Husband" on pages 114-118. Choose seven of them and put one into practice each day. For example, if you choose "greet him with enthusiasm when he comes home"—do that! Make it extra special...maybe even over the top with a sign on the door greeting him and a hug and a long kiss upon seeing him!

Prayer for the Wise Wife

Heavenly Father, we come before you and praise you that your Word gives us clear direction on our role as a helper. Jesus, we ask that you speak to each of us individually and that you convict us and lead us to where we may be missing out on your best in this role. We know that you are faithful and that you will reveal to us how we can serve our husbands most effectively as an overflow of our relationship with you and you alone. Jesus, we count it an honor to be a wife who is glorifying you in our role and ask that you continue to nurture us, guide us, and lead us in this role. Help others to see a reflection of you in us as we choose to respect, honor, and submit to you and our spouse. Keep our hearts soft and free from bitterness and resentment. Show us what you would have us do in our marriages each and every day. We love you, Lord! Amen.

Prayer for Your Husband

Lord Jesus, I come before you and lift my husband up to you. Jesus, I ask that you guide him into growing and developing into the role of leader of our family. I ask that you place godly men in his life to walk with him as he continues to mature.

Give him great examples of what headship and Christian leadership really mean. Help him to turn toward you, and may he seek you all the days of his life. As a result, may our marriage be a reflection of you. In your precious and holy name, amen.

GRATITUDE

* * * * * * * * * * * * * * * * * * * *

*It is not joy that makes us grateful; it is
gratitude that makes us joyful.*

DAVID STEINDL-RAST

Who doesn't like to hear the words *thank you*? I know I sure do. Yet sometimes I begin to take Greg for granted and become negligent of the frequent expression of gratitude. It's important for me to express to my husband what I appreciate about him and the things he does for me and our family.

When Greg was in India on a mission trip, it was easy to see all that he does for me and for our family, how he helps around the house, and how he just calms the entire place down. But when he's here every day, it's easy to take him for granted.

This is a common occurrence in marriages. Once couples move through the honeymoon phase, they can go from appreciating and loving every little detail about each other to failing to appreciate all the other person adds to their life.

Amie Gordon, a psychologist from UC Berkeley, blames this for the downfall of many relationships. According to her work, it's easy to simply get accustomed to having your spouse in your life...and along the way, you forget why you chose to be with them. We become deadened to our spouse's special qualities and instead focus on things that annoy us about them. This can leave couples confused and discouraged. As Dr. Gordon puts it, "Maybe the man they married isn't so great after all...What happened to the spark in our relationship?"[1]

The power of gratitude is real. If you are wondering about your marriage and asking what happened to the feelings you used to have, I encourage you to start practicing the habit of gratitude.

When talking with another mom, she shared, "I just don't have any feelings for him anymore." The encouragement I offered her is exactly what I will say here: Look for things you can be grateful for! Ladies, we have to fight for our marriages and be intentional with what we can do to lead our hearts back toward our husbands. Now, I'm not dismissing hurt feelings or difficult scenarios, but I'm encouraging all of us to do something simple that works even in difficult seasons. Our marital satisfaction will increase because of two simple words: *thank you.*

> *Give thanks in all circumstances; for this*
> *is God's will for you in Christ Jesus.*
> 1 THESSALONIANS 5:18 NIV

Right before Greg left on his extended mission trip, he hung a light fixture in the dining room for me. If you had been there, you might have thought he'd bought me a new diamond ring by my response. I *love* the new light fixture! I've hated the light fixtures in this house since we moved in more than five years ago. I found two fixtures I liked online, and Greg ordered them for me. When they arrived, I figured they would sit in the box until I called an electrician to install them. To my great surprise, I woke up one Saturday morning (because he also let me sleep in) to find Greg removing the old dining room fixture and putting up one of the new ones! What a gift to be able to flip the switch and see my new light fixture shine. Every day he was in India, I walked by and switched the light on—day or night—just because it was a sweet reminder of what he did for me!

But how many times have I allowed an opportunity to thank him pass by without a word? Apparently I'm not alone on this one! Sadly, we often feel more gratitude and thankfulness in response to strangers' acts of kindness than our own family members'. I say thank you to the Starbucks lady, have total understanding (well, at least most times) if she doesn't get my order correct, and then even thank her when she gets it right! Do I always show that much grace to my own husband?

Scientists at the University of Georgia asked more than 200 couples questions about their partner and their relationship, and they found that gratitude is the best predictor of how happy someone is in their marriage.[2] This shows the power of *thank you*. Even if a couple is experiencing distress and difficulty in other areas, gratitude in the relationship can help promote positive marital outcomes. Saying thank you could also help mitigate damage caused from past arguments.

So let's sharpen up our gratitude skills and express it as often as we can.

How to Show Gratitude

> *Gratitude can transform common days into*
> *thanksgivings, turn routine jobs into joy, and*
> *change ordinary opportunities into blessings.*
> WILLIAM ARTHUR WARD

Now, you may be thinking, "How hard is it to simply thank my husband for doing something?" Well, according to the research, we are struggling with this! Whatever is hindering us—maybe pride, busyness, or conflict—let's examine a few simple steps that will teach us to really build our gratitude skills in our marriages.

Focus on His Value

You will never show gratitude to someone you don't value. We must embrace all that we appreciate about our husbands. Remember that list you made back in chapter 2? Refer to it often to remember your favorite things about your husband's personality and character traits! We are called to value others above ourselves in God's Word— so why not start with our husbands?

> *Do nothing out of selfish ambition or vain conceit.*
> *Rather, in humility value others above yourself.*
> PHILIPPIANS 2:3 NIV

Look for What He Does Right

> *Encourage one another daily.*
> HEBREWS 3:13 NIV

As we are watching for things to thank him for, we begin to see him in a more positive light. Philippians 4:8 reminds us to "fix [our] thoughts on what is true, and honorable, and right, and pure, and lovely, and admirable. Think about things that are excellent and worthy of praise" (NLT). This is a powerful thing to do! I know that as I begin watching for even one thing every day to thank Greg for, I notice all kinds of things. I gave myself the challenge of thanking him before we went to bed every night, and wouldn't you know, that list wrote itself. I would lie down at the end of the day and say, "Now how long have you been emptying the dishwasher every day and also folding laundry? Did you just start doing these things?"

And of course he hadn't. He had been doing them for weeks. But I never slowed down enough to really look and watch for what he was doing. Instead, I saw only the things he wasn't doing.

My new challenge is to find at least five things Greg does each day to thank him for. Now I have to write them down, or I forget! My daily practice in gratitude has impacted me as well. I now recognize what a servant's heart Greg truly has, and I can hardly believe I was oblivious to it for many years.

I asked Greg and a few other men in our small group how they felt when their wives expressed gratitude. I wanted to know what gratitude did for them personally. The responses definitely backed up what all the research says about the overall impact of gratitude on a marriage. Greg said, "It makes me feel successful as a husband. It's like you're giving me a job performance evaluation and saying that I pass. It means that you've noticed that I'm trying to do good things for you and our family. You're saying that I have what it takes because I did something right. Relationally, it makes me lean in and draw close to you. Gratitude is such a connector! I feel really respected and loved because you took the time to point out what you appreciate."

Another husband in our group said, "It's a rare person who doesn't thrive in an atmosphere of support and appreciation. People flourish in a wave of recognition of effort and sacrifice. Often my wife will send me a text when I'm on call at the hospital. It means the world to me and keeps me going. Our daughter also texts me and encourages me when she knows I'm gone. It all means the world to me, and I would always love to receive more of it!"

Choose Gratitude

> *Every time I think of you, I give thanks to my God.*
> PHILIPPIANS 1:3 NLT

Share specific things that your spouse did that you are thankful for. Gratitude is a choice and a discipline. Choosing gratitude has amazing benefits for us personally, but also for those we love. This choice keeps us humble because we are recognizing our blessings. Our posture is one of seeing how blessed we are by our spouses.

We benefit both emotionally and physiologically from positive thinking. The opposite is also true—negativity impacts our brains and can lead to depression and anxiety. Grateful people

> are happier
> are more resilient
> are less depressed
> have higher self-esteem
> have better relationships
> have regular and lower heart rhythms
> get better sleep

Gratitude is an attitude that comes from the habit of giving thanks. Practice this habit regularly in your home, in your relationships, and especially in your marriage.

Offer a Compliment

Don't forget to compliment your husband for the effort he puts forth in your marriage—with the way he parents the kids, folds the laundry extra neatly, or cooks an amazing meal. Don't let the compliments he receives come from others—let yours be the first compliment he hears each day and the last he hears before he goes to sleep. Offer compliments both in public and private.

Serve Him with Acts of Kindness

Whether you are taking out the trash, dropping off lunch, or picking up the dry cleaning, my mantra in all relationships is "give them what you desire." The same is true in marriage. If you aren't receiving a lot of gratitude, dish out the words *thank you* and surprise your spouse with small acts of kindness. Who knows what will happen! When spouses receive gratitude from their loved one, they are more likely to give it back.

Whatever you do, whether in word or deed, do it all in the name of the Lord Jesus, giving thanks to God the Father through him.
COLOSSIANS 3:17 NIV

Be Creative!

It's always nice to say the two magic words "thank you." However, change it up regularly. Leave notes of thankfulness, buy a card or a small gift, or buy him his favorite coffee on your way home. Greg came home from work one day and handed me a card thanking me for working so hard both at Focus on the Family and on this book. Tears streamed down my face as I read his sweet words—especially when a gift card to my favorite store fell on the floor! He was stunned by my tears—Greg thought he had said something wrong. But the truth was his words, his act of kindness, and his acknowledgment of my hard work meant so much to me, it brought me to tears!

Where your treasure is, there your heart will be also.
MATTHEW 6:21 NIV

When we notice positive behavior and blessings in our life, our heart is then drawn toward those things—like our spouse! And that's a great thing for any marriage. Don't be afraid to tell your husband you are grateful or that you noticed when he did something admirable. In doing so your husband will recognize that you are watching and noticing the effort he is putting forth, and his heart will be impacted as well as yours.

We can only be said to be alive in those moments
when our hearts are conscious of our treasures.
THORNTON WILDER

Practice Gratitude Regularly with God

Gratitude should be practiced in every healthy relationship. Don't forget to be intentional about thanking the Lord. While on a walk with my daughter Annie, she said, "How can we be so blessed to live in this beautiful place with beautiful walking paths?" Her question blew me away. As a result of my work on this project, I was already trying to be more intentional about practicing gratitude not just in my marriage, but in life in general. Annie's words felt like an instant wake-up call. I seized the opportunity to tell Annie what else I was grateful for—including our family, our friends, our neighbors who had recently moved in, and yes, even the beauty of Colorado. Get into the habit of offering the Lord a few compliments too!

In the Psalms, David did this regularly.

> Make a joyful noise to the LORD, all the earth! Serve the LORD with gladness! Come into his presence with singing! Know that the LORD, he is God! It is he who made us, and we are his; we are his people, and the sheep of his pasture. Enter his gates with thanksgiving, and his courts with praise! Give thanks to him; bless his name! For the LORD is good; his steadfast love endures forever, and his faithfulness to all generations (Psalm 100:1-5 ESV).

Our 19-year-old daughter, Murphy, spent last semester in Beijing, China, working at our youngest daughter's former orphanage. Murphy had an amazing experience doing a medical internship and loving on sweet babies, and she also gained amazing insight about gratitude. She sent me a text late one night that said, "God has gone from being a big, powerful presence up in heaven to my intimate friend, walking right beside me. As I've spent more time alone and out of my comfort zone this semester in China, I have begun noticing the little things that "my friend" does for me. I've been keeping a list of "the little things" and as I've done this for three months, I realize now that I'm more content and joyful than I've ever been. Before coming here, I was waiting for God to do the "big" things in my life and now I just simply say "thank you" for the little things He does for me—each and every day." Now that's gratitude.

Throughout the Psalms, David was continually offering gratitude to God regardless of what he faced. He always relied on the truth of who God is and His goodness—throughout his trials and blessings. This choice to have an attitude of gratitude carried him through difficult scenarios. The more we focus and reflect on God's goodness and practice gratitude no matter the circumstances, the more it will become habit and naturally flow out of a heart that loves Him.

> *I will give thanks to the LORD with my whole heart;*
> *I will recount all of your wonderful deeds.*
> PSALM 9:1 ESV

What Season Are You In?

As you contemplate having a heart of gratitude, reflect on what season you are currently in—especially in your marriage. Remember, we all have seasons of mountaintop highs and valley lows we think will never end. If you happen to be in one of those challenging seasons (and believe me, I've been there too), I encourage you to practice gratitude toward your husband. This is a choice you can make without him knowing or even responding. Sure, it's nice when we receive gratitude; however, the only person that we can control is ourselves.

Think about what an amazing gift it would be to thank your husband each and every night for something that he did for you in the last 24 hours. What an encouragement and wonderful way to drift off to sleep. I love it when Greg falls asleep on a positive note at the end of a long day. Although I cannot control his state of mind, as his wife, I can sure influence it, and I cannot imagine any man, husband, or person, for that matter, rejecting a heartfelt "thank you."

A Challenge

After learning that our men desire to receive gratitude, I challenged my social media followers to complete the following statement: *I am thankful for my husband because…*

I received many wonderful responses and found myself smiling all day long as I read them. Seeing women willing to share their deep gratitude for their husbands made my heart happy. Here are some of the responses:

> "I'm grateful for my husband because he shows me love, kindness, and adores me. He lifts me up when I'm down, still flirts with me on ordinary days, and calls me out when my attitude and words are unbecoming." —Sherri

> "He loves the Lord…very involved in civic duty (which is rare), and brings out the best in me." —Heidi

> "Through my relationship with him, I've had the opportunity to experience the pursuit God has for me and to get a sweet taste of the new beginnings, the forgiveness, the grace, and the reconciliation Jesus offers." —Amy

"He is supportive and we love to learn and live together."
—Amy

"He loves me and cares for me—always has and always will." —Nancy

"He challenges me to be the best me…he selflessly works his tail off to allow me to be at home and then still finds the energy to help out at home when he is off. He chooses to love the things about me that should drive him crazy, and he is quick to apologize even when he doesn't have to. He is the same person whether he is at work as a physician or at home as a husband and dad. He teaches our boys respect by loving us like he does, and the most important trait is his love for the Lord. He always tries to make me feel beautiful, even when I'm in a frumpy mood." —Susan

"He purposely chose jobs that would give him family time and lots of it. He is a high school coach and teaches just to be with us! Priceless." —Kim

"He's a goal setter and a goal achiever. He loves me on my most unlovable days. He drives me to the brink of crazy and brings me back to reality on a wild ride. His priority in life is to love God and love others. It's a rocky relationship at times, but a smooth relationship would be ordinary. He's also great at washing dishes." —Stephanie

How about you? How would you finish this prompt?

QUESTIONS FOR REFLECTION

Were you surprised to learn the importance of gratitude and how it impacts us and our relationships?

As you reflect on your relationship with your husband, is it difficult for you to express gratitude to him? Why or why not? Or maybe it's easy for you—what helps you do this?

CHALLENGE

What are you grateful for that your husband does for you or your family? How can you creatively express your gratitude every day? Keep a running list of things you see him doing each day. At the end of the day, before bed, bless him by saying thank you for something specific. For example, I would say, "Greg, I cannot tell you how much it meant to me that you were willing to take Annie to soccer practice today. You sat there for two hours while she practiced and took that time away from your schedule. Thank you so much for serving our family in that way." Now it's your turn!

Prayer for the Wise Wife

Lord, I come before you and ask you to give me eyes to see the amazing gift you gave me when you gave me my husband. There are many things he does to help me, support me, and love me and our family. Help me to notice these things regularly and to also take time to express gratitude. The simple words thank you *have such a big impact on anyone— but especially in a marriage. Lord, in your Word, gratitude is a main theme. It is talked about over 162 times. We are commanded to "give thanks." Help me to have a grateful heart toward you, Lord—but also help me to express it more to my husband. In your precious and holy name, amen.*

Prayer for Your Husband

Lord, once again I lift my husband up to you. Jesus, help him to have a grateful heart—not only toward me, but most importantly toward you, Lord. Help him to see the blessings you have given him each and every day. And Lord, as I am being more intentional about thanking him and expressing gratitude, help him to do the same in return. Although I cannot make him return the effort, Jesus, your Holy Spirit can lead him to have a heart that is bubbling over with gratefulness. Lord, I thank you for the gift of my husband and ask that you watch over him and keep him. In Jesus' precious name, amen.

YOUR INFLUENCE

A wife of noble character is her husband's crown, but
a disgraceful wife is like decay in his bones.

PROVERBS 12:4 NIV

My friend Julie told me her influence over her husband extends to their use of expired coupons on date nights. After seeing the confused look on my face, she explained that when she presents an expired coupon for a restaurant, she playfully begs the server, "We have four very small children, and we may never have the opportunity to be with each other alone in public again." She says she makes her plea as she wipes dried spit-up off her shoulder, and it works every time! "The best part," she says, "is that Mark is now the one who begs for mercy when our coupon has expired—I've actually taught him something!"

We all have something to teach one another, and as wives we can use our knowledge and skills to influence our husbands. It might be the art of using expired coupons like Julie, or maybe it's along the lines of how to handle money, interact with the kids, or pursue meaningful friendships.

Our choices and behavior have enormous influence over our husbands' lives. Whether we recognize it or not, everything we do has the potential to influence our spouse for either good or ill.

However, when we become aware of the ways we can influence others and we become intentional with our behavior, we never know what the outcome will be! If we choose to behave in ways to positively influence our spouses, we may find we get positive behavior in return.

Research Backs This Up...

As we embrace our ability to influence our husbands, research shows it's also beneficial for our husbands to be positively influenced by us. In a long-term study of 130 newlywed couples, Dr. John Gottman discovered that men who allow their wives to influence them have happier marriages and are less likely to divorce.[1]

Married men are positively influenced by their wives and marriage in the following ways:

- *They make more money.* A Virginia Commonwealth University study found that married men earn 22 percent more than their similarly experienced but single colleagues.[2]

- *Being married speeds up the next promotion.* Married men receive higher performance ratings and faster promotions than bachelors, a 2005 study of US Navy officers reported.[3]

- *Women often keep men out of trouble.* According to a recent US Department of Justice report, male victims of violent crime are nearly four times more likely to be single than married.[4]

- *Married men are more satisfied in bed.* In 2006, British researchers reviewed the sexual habits of men in 38 countries and found that in every country, married men have more sex.[5]

• *Married men have a better chance of surviving cancer.* In a Norwegian study, divorced and never-married male cancer patients had higher mortality rates than married men.[6]

• *Married men live longer.* A UCLA study found that people in generally excellent health were 88 percent more likely to die over the eight-year study period if they were single.[7]

Based on these studies, it sure seems we influence our husbands just by being around. However, as we talked about in chapter 3, we are created differently—male and female. Our differences as women can influence our men in amazing ways. And yes, the inverse is true—they can influence us as well (in case there are any men reading this).

Influential Women of the Bible

I love looking at the amazing women in the Bible. Many were women of influence and made an impact through their might, courage, and behavior! The culture wasn't one that supported women's rights, yet there are over 14,000 words spoken in Scripture by 93 specific women.[8] And many of these women had amazing impact and influence that ultimately changed history and the world.

Think about these biblical ladies:

• Deborah was a judge in a day and age when women weren't known as judges. She held great political and military positions and was seen as a warrior, prophet, and judge. She influenced through love for her people, leading them to victory, hearing God's voice, and step-ping on to the front lines of battle.

- The Proverbs 31 lady defied all odds as she was a suc-cessful businesswoman in a time when women weren't CEOs and vice presidents of corporations. She provides an example in Scripture for women all over the world to live by. She also models how to influence others through her teaching and ultimately encourages other women to influence the world.

- Women weren't seen as useful, yet Mary bore Jesus as a young teenager.

- Esther, an orphan, became a queen and played an important role in saving the Jewish people.

One of my favorite stories of a biblical woman of influence is Abigail. She was married to a man named Nabal, a wealthy land-owner, who was preparing for a celebration with large amounts of food and drink during sheep-shearing season. David sent ten of his men to make the request for food for himself and his men with the promise of safeguarding Nabal's property and livestock. Nabal arro-gantly exploded and refused. Enraged, David ordered four hundred of his men to go with him to kill Nabal and his entire household.

Enter Abigail. She hears the news from one of Nabal's servants prior to David's arrival. Immediately, she springs into action and prepares the food requested. She loads two hundred loaves of bread, two hundred cakes of figs, and other delicious snacks into a caravan. The amazing thing about this woman is that she positions herself in the front, leading the caravan!

When Abigail comes face-to-face with David, she begs him to forgive her husband, Nabal. She not only begs for mercy, but she presents the excellent food she prepared for David and his men. Her presence calms David, who ultimately changes his mind about destroying Nabal and his household.

Upon Abigail's arrival back home, she finds her husband intoxicated. Abigail wisely waits until morning to tell Nabal of her talk with David. Upon hearing her news, Nabal turns ghostly white and his heart dies; he passes away ten days later.

Soon David sends for Abigail and tells her his desire to marry her. As a widow, Abigail knows her best choice is to marry David, but she also knows he is an amazing man of God. The two marry and later have a son—Daniel.

Abigail was courageous under pressure. She had other options, yet she chose to protect her husband, regardless of his behavior, and also their household. She acted with wisdom and clarity and didn't go down the road of being a victim, hiding, and protecting herself, and she had great spiritual discernment. Truly, she could have put responsibility on her husband and said, "This isn't my problem—it's his." With her husband's drinking issues and haughty attitude, likely no one would have blamed her. But she didn't. She knew David was a man of God and that the Lord had called him to be a leader in Israel, so she chose to intervene in the situation.

Abigail is just one of many women in Scripture we can learn from. They all courageously chose to impact their cultures, their communities, and, yes, even their husbands.

Historical Wives of Influence

We can learn not only from the example of biblical women, but from wives in our own country's history. Many women supported and influenced their husbands, ultimately shaping the course of our nation.

Coretta Scott King married Martin Luther King Jr. in 1953. She asked that the part of the vows asking her to *obey* her husband be removed. This small detail is an example of the independent streak that characterized Coretta. She was a supportive wife who believed wholeheartedly in her husband's mission, yet she was also a woman who took action.

She became deeply involved in causes of racial justice and nonviolent change. She was at Dr. King's side throughout the key events of the Civil Rights Movement, and she lobbied hard to see the Civil Rights Act of 1964 passed. She worked hand in hand with Dr. King until he was assassinated on April 4, 1968.

Other inspiring women include...

- Eleanor Roosevelt, who stepped in to support her husband when he contracted polio. She filled in at his scheduled appearances and speeches, where she spoke passionately on race discrimination and women's rights. She lectured, wrote daily newspaper columns, appeared on the radio programming, and held press conferences.

- Abigail Adams had a unique relationship of influence with her husband, John. When John was away fulfilling his political duties, Abigail filled him in on community matters and advised him on political matters. Abigail continuously urged her husband to enforce laws that were supportive of women. John consulted her about the daily matters of his political work.

- Harriet Beecher Stowe raised seven children and in her spare time wrote a book that changed the course of American history. She and her husband, Calvin, a minister, couldn't tolerate the institution of slavery. They both became active in the Underground Railroad and helped many slaves to freedom. Harriet was inspired to write *Uncle Tom's Cabin* by an experience she had with a dying slave.

These women of influence inspire me in my journey to be a wife of influence. My hope is you too will find inspiration in the lives of these women and others, not to make you think, "I need to be doing more," or to send you to any of the guilt-ridden places we go in our minds. I want to inspire you to embrace your influence in your marriage and in your world—much like Abigail and Esther did, and like Eleanor and Harriet too. They each took advantage of God-given opportunities with great courage and responsibility, and instead of trembling with fear or filling their minds with self-doubt, they took action that ultimately allowed them to influence, encourage, inspire, persuade, and counsel their husbands. As you can see, their actions (sometimes even in the form of words) had profound impact—yet nothing any one of them did would be unattainable in this day and age. They were ordinary women, living ordinary lives, but they stirred their husbands to reach their potential.

We have discussed our God-given role in marriage as a "helpmate." These great biblical women and women in history were also helpers. But Scripture is also filled with women who used their influence not for good, but for harm. Think of these women:

- Eve: Her first bite of forbidden fruit ushered sin into the world. She gave the fruit of the tree of knowledge of good and evil to her husband to eat and so became an agent of temptation for Adam.

- Jezebel: Her name means "chaste, free from carnal connection." She was left to be remembered as "the wicked woman" because that was the life she chose to live. She

persecuted the saints, had no fear of man or God, and
she maintained idolatry in all of its splendor. In the end,
she was thrown from a high balcony by her own eunuchs
and died. And then her body was eaten by hunting dogs.

- Lot's daughters: They were desperate to have children,
so with no other males around, they seduced their own
father with wine and then slept with him.

- Peninnah: She had a wicked, sharp tongue that she used
whenever her own heart was hurting. She was caught in
the middle of a painful love triangle with her husband,
Elkanah, and his other wife, Hannah (whom he loved
more).

- Maacah: She was married to King Solomon's eldest son,
Rehoboam. Eventually, she became the Queen Mother
and she restored the old religion—worship of the fertil-
ity gods Baal and Asherah. She ended up living out the
last days of her life in a claustrophobic harem after being
removed from the throne.

- Athaliah: She was daughter of Ahab (one of the worst
kings of Israel) and daughter of Jezebel, the most wicked
queen in the Bible. She spread idolatry and became
queen by slaughtering the rest of the royal family, including her own grandchildren. She ended up being executed
outside the gate of the temple in Jerusalem.

- Sapphira: Sapphira and her husband, Ananias, lied
about the money they had given to Peter, God, and the
people. She and Ananias both dropped dead in front of
Peter.

Sadly, there are many more women of the Bible that used their influence for harm. It's obvious that we get to choose to use our influence for good or evil.

As you reflect on your current circumstances, what is one thing you can do to be a woman and wife of positive influence? Will you hide in fear, embrace the victim role, or doubt your ability to the point of doing nothing? Or will you embrace the role God has given you to use your influence for good? History might not remember us, and we may not be found in Internet searches for women of positive influence (although you never know), but our impact will be found in the everyday lives of our husbands, children, and friends. Our fingerprints will be found everywhere; however, most importantly, we will be found faithful by our heavenly Father. I'm inspired—how about you?

Years ago, while traveling home from Dallas, Texas, Greg called to tell me he'd run into the Focus on the Family president, Jim Daly, at the airport. When Greg approached him, Jim said, "I can't believe I'm running into you! I was just thinking about you and Erin." When he learned they were headed to the same destination, Jim asked Greg to meet him for breakfast the next morning to discuss a potential opportunity.

On the phone, Greg told me he would have sworn that Jim was interviewing him for a job. My first reaction was to say, "Don't even meet with Jim Daly, because we aren't going to move." We had just returned from China after completing the adoption process for our daughter Annie. She was traumatized and so were the rest of us! It had been a crazy, long ordeal to get her home, and getting her settled was taking much longer than I ever expected. However, with a willingness to allow my husband to influence me, I agreed to pray about the meeting, and we agreed Greg should meet Jim for breakfast.

At the meeting, Greg learned his gut instinct was accurate, and in fact Jim wanted us to both come to work at Focus on the Family. Although my heart was weary, I agreed to continue praying about this possible adventure and allow my husband to influence me in this area. That decision has turned into a five-year tenure at Focus. We pray it will last many more years.

In the same way you would love for your husband to be influenced by you, are you also willing to be influenced by him? This position is one of respect, humility, and honor. The choice to allow your husband to influence you can lead to an increased overall happiness in your marriage relationship. And when your husband experiences your response to his influence, he may be more open to being influenced by you as well.

We've all heard, "Behind every great man there is a great woman." I couldn't agree more. Often when there is a success story for a man, there is a wonderfully amazing wife supporting, encouraging, and rooting him on from the background.

Five Practical Ways to Influence Your Husband

Women transform male lust into love; channel male wanderlust into jobs, homes and families; link men to specific children; rear children into citizens; change hunters into fathers; divert male will to power into a drive to create. Women conceive the future that men tend to flee.
GEORGE GILDER

God had a purpose in creating men and women differently. Our differences bring a beautiful balance to our marriages. Our differences also provide us opportunities to teach our husbands. By embracing our femininity and not downplaying it in the way our culture often encourages, we can have a positive influence on our husbands in everyday, practical ways:

Be His Relationship Mentor

In discussing the topic of relationship mentors with a group of men and women, several men were offended by the idea. I explained my premise that there are things both men and women can learn from each other. This is not intended to be offensive—simply true. I assured the men this wasn't about "why women are better than men." It is about our natural strengths and how we can use them to influence our husbands. (Men will have to wait for the book on what every wife needs from her husband!)

Women were created with a relational mindset—even the introverts. We were created to connect with lots of people. Connecting is part of our nature. God created us with a wicked sense of relational intuition and understanding of relationships that our husbands can greatly benefit from. Men typically don't have the same capacity for relationship building that we do. We thrive with many connections in our lives and typically do a pretty good job balancing them (although they can cause problems if out of balance or mishandled). We can easily encourage our husbands to pursue male friends and relationships with family members, simply in the way we model relationship building in our daily lives. It may not seem like much, but the impact can lead to a stronger relationship between a mother and son or between a father and son.

Help Him Reach His Greatest Potential

A wife can use her influence in powerful ways to encourage and motivate her husband.

The first settlers to cross the Atlantic and arrive at Jamestown, Virginia, in 1607 consisted of 200 rugged individuals. All men. Without any women among them, the men struggled to survive in the New World.

According to Gail Collins, author of *America's Women,* without women present, the men weren't very productive.[9] They had no real motivation to work hard and provide. It was good enough for them to produce just enough for themselves. When the women did finally arrive beginning in 1608, Collins described the female settlers as being "marooned in what must have seemed like a long, rowdy fraternity party, minus food."[10] One new settler arrived in 1611 and wrote that he found the men engaged in "their daily and usual workes, bowling in the streets."[11] But soon the women became wives. The tide of apathy began to turn. Within a few decades, the colonies, thanks to the influence of women, were flourishing.

So, what happened? I think it's pretty obvious. Marriage inspired a ragtag group of men to help lay the foundation for our nation. Women—wives in particular—were seen as the stabilizing and key ingredient. The women of Jamestown teach us that no society can thrive without women, and certainly not without women who are partners in strong and healthy marriages. Without wives to care and provide for, the men of Jamestown were content to drift and simply get by. It was the institution of marriage that provided them with incentive to work, build, and create a new society.

Women influence a man's productivity and desire to achieve just by making a man a husband. We bring motivation that can encourage them to reach their potential, whether this shows up in working more or working smarter, getting the promotion, or striving for a higher level in their career. When a man gets married, he takes on a new identity of provider, impacting how he shows up in life—including in his work and achievement. Married men have the added benefit of receiving advice and encouragement from a wise wife.

The influence that we have is seen not just in our husband's achievements at work, but also in many other areas of his life. One way I influence Greg is through encouraging him in the area of his appearance. I often give Greg fashion feedback such as, "Hey, babe, looks like you could use a haircut!" Or more recently, encouraging him to color his graying hair.

After reading all of this, you may find yourself thinking, "Sure, that's what it looks like in your life—not mine. My husband doesn't come home after work—instead he hangs out with the guys." Or maybe you are thinking, "My husband isn't motivated to work and hasn't held a job in a year." Or perhaps, "My husband wouldn't let me pick out any of his clothes if his life depended on it." I'm guessing all of these scenarios are difficult and painful for you as a wife, and I encourage you to not nag, berate, or criticize your husband as a result. Your husband may or may not accept your influence—whether it is your words or your actions—and the thing you must remember is you *cannot* make your husband accept your influence. The more you push, the more he will try to escape. Our influence can be used for good to empower or persuade, but we don't get to decide if it does any of those things at all. I encourage you to influence your husband to reach his potential by making sure you are acknowledging the complete picture of who he is and what he *has* done in your marriage. And then turn to the one who can influence his heart—Jesus.

> Our influence can be used for good to empower or persuade, but we don't get to decide if it does any of those things at all.

Mary Kassian puts it, "A positive influencer knows that ultimately it is God, and not she, who effects positive change in a person's life. So she relies on Him and on her most potent, influential tool—prayer."[12]

Use your influence for good, not harm—remember you are his wife, not his mother, his career coach, or his fashion designer. Pray about how God wants you to encourage, inspire, and motivate your husband through your love and presence in his life. Or the Lord may lead you to set some firm boundaries in order to bring about change. I know there are some of you reading this who have tried and tried and tried to influence—with no resolution. In love, it may be time to say "no more—we need to try something different." Pray and seek God's leading. Enlist the help of others—either a Christian counselor or pastor, or call 1-800-A-FAMILY. It may look different than how we imagine it—but trust God that His ways are best.

Help Him Understand the Mind of a Woman

Although this isn't the case for all couples, often women are able to connect with their emotions more easily. Even men who are in touch with their emotions sometimes have difficulty expressing them. They have been trained from a young age to not express these in fear of being too soft or effeminate. After talking to many couples, I have found the female is usually able to express her feelings more freely, although she has also received cultural messages that tell her her emotions are a result of being too dramatic or hormonal.

We have an opportunity to give our husbands permission to express heartfelt emotions safely in our marriages. If your husband has never expressed his emotions openly, it may be a bit awkward for him. This is where you come in! You can model expressing emotions by talking freely about yours. You can encourage him by having probing conversations about how he is feeling.

When I asked the couples in our small group about how wives influence their husbands, I got a variety of responses. Here's what a few of the ladies had to say:

- "I ask questions to help him get to the heart of the matter. I help to draw him out into the depth of the situation."

- "When one of us is going through a lot, the other steps

in and carries the other through the difficult seasons. We are there for each other in helping the other express what they are feeling—whether that be me or him. We are together in this relationship, always striving to be open and fully vulnerable with each other."

- "With the stress of his job, often he isn't able to handle my level of emotion. He is so emotionally spent when he gets home, and that makes it difficult for him to deal with my stress. Therefore, I often try to focus on his emotions and helping him express those effectively."

One powerful lesson you can help your husband learn is how to respond to tears. A woman's emotional response can freak men out. They often don't know what to do with us! It helps if we can tell them what we need. Their natural tendency is to jump in and try to fix the problem. The truth is there isn't always a problem to fix. We may just need to express our emotion in order to sort things out. Your husband might try to move you through the emotion because he is uncomfortable with your tears and feels out of control. It's no secret that men get frustrated when they can't figure out women's emotions. The following explains some of what's behind this:

Research has found that men have more difficulty identifying facial expressions than women do, especially those on the female face. Men are also less skilled at identifying nonverbal cues of sadness and fear. Unfortunately, women tend to use a lot of facial expressions to communicate, which can lead to frustrating situations for you both: You feel that your needs are being ignored, while he's exasperated by the subtlety of your expressions and body language.[13]

Be willing to explain what is going on emotionally with you when either of you are feeling frustration. I encourage you to wait until emotions have simmered down, but don't miss out on the opportunity to coach your husband about your emotional response. Often, this will translate into changes in his interactions with other women and may help him grow his emotional intelligence.

Help Him Be a Better Dad

Since women are typically highly equipped with empathy and compassion, we can assist our husbands in the fatherhood department as well. I remember when our kids were young, if they got hurt in any manner, they would scream for mom. They would bypass Greg altogether! It offended him until he started watching how I reacted when the children ran to me. He saw me comfort them emotionally and physically, validate their pain, care for their wounds, and encourage them to get back out there if they weren't too injured. As he observed me, he realized he usually skipped everything I did and went straight to telling them to get back out there! Greg changed his approach and is proud to say that the kids now seek us out equally for comfort.

Additionally, Greg has learned I often connect with our now older children however they allow me to. We have two older daughters. Murphy is nineteen and Taylor is twenty-two, and they call me more frequently than they call Greg. After analyzing what I do, he noticed that I go to great lengths to take their calls regardless of the time of day or how busy I am. Although talking on the phone isn't my favorite activity, I have learned to enjoy it because it means staying connected to my daughters. I can also explain to Greg what the girls might be going through and how he can better connect with them. He now tries to make more of an effort to call them regularly, and my husband who despises texting has taken it up to connect with our girls!

As moms we have many opportunities to encourage our husbands' success as dads. We influence how our children view their dads by how we talk about them in their absence. Praise your husband however you can in front of the children. They pick up on how you talk about their father and are more likely to see their daddy in a positive light when it's first modeled by you. Encourage your husband in any way you can when he makes an effort to connect with the kids or spend time with them.

There may be other ways you can help your husband succeed as a dad, so be intentional about following through when you notice something particular to your situation.

We influence our men in countless ways. They make more money, live longer, are healthier, and are even more satisfied sexually all because they chose to marry us. Ladies, we have quite an impact, and when we are willing to take action in order to encourage, influence, and cheer our husbands on, the possibilities are endless.

She brings him good, not harm, all the days of her life.
PROVERBS 31:12 NIV

QUESTIONS FOR REFLECTION

Before reading this chapter, were you aware of the benefits researchers have found married men enjoy as a result of simply being married? Do any of them surprise you?

What is one way you have influenced your husband since you married? If you are brave, go to him and ask him how he thinks you have influenced him.

On the flip side, think about ways in which your husband has influenced you. How has he helped make you a better wife, mom, or woman?

Lastly, how have you influenced each other as a couple? How has your marriage encouraged you both to achieve your very best "inner self" and "outer self"?

. . . .
CHALLENGE
. . . .

Spend some time praying and asking the Lord where you need to take action in your marriage. Review some of the stories of the women in the Bible (not the women who used their influence for harm) or the great influential women in history, and reflect on any opportunity you have to come alongside your husband and influence his journey in a positive way. This week, make sure you come up with one practical way to influence him positively. For example, if he has a big meeting or event, help him pick out his outfit. Take it to the dry cleaner so it's fully pressed and looking good.

Prayer for the Wise Wife

O Lord Jesus, I ask that you give me wisdom and discernment around my level of influence in my husband's life. I want to influence him for good and not harm. Help me to see where I can encourage him or how I can guide him. He has influence on me as well; help me to be receptive to his leading. Lord, help me to take action when I need to take action. Help me to be strong and courageous as so many women have modeled in Scripture and in history. I thank you for how you made us different, male and female, and how we can beautifully encourage one another to become more like you, Jesus. Amen.

Prayer for Your Husband

Jesus, I thank you for the gift of my husband. I thank you that he is so very different than I am. Help him to be open to my influence and even more importantly, Lord, your influence. Help him to turn to me when he needs me—help him to not be resistant to asking for help. Help him to see how much I love him and how I do want to be that woman behind him, cheering him on to be the very best man of God that he can be. Jesus, infuse him with your wisdom, strength, and discernment. In Jesus' name, amen.

9

TIME TO REJUVENATE

I pray that you... know this love that surpasses knowledge—
that you may be filled to the measure of all the fullness of God.

EPHESIANS 3:17,19 NIV

One topic in marriage can be an argument waiting to happen. Bring up free time and who needs it more—a husband or a wife—and it's a surefire way to initiate a heated discussion! I encourage you to recognize you both need unallocated time alone. We need to encourage one another in our marriages to take time to reignite our hearts. We all have "those" days when we need a break!

Recently when I was overdue for "me" time, I felt a need to get out of the house as quickly as possible. Although I should have kept my bottom firmly planted in the chair in order to keep writing, I chose my well-being (and frankly, everyone else's in the house). I just had to have a break. Our nine-year-old daughter Annie had just had yet another procedure on her palate—CT scans, pulled teeth, orthodontics, surgery—and I had spent days and weeks dealing with both Annie's anxiousness and my own. After surgery, I devoted all of my energy and attention to my sweet, swollen, chipmunk-faced little girl who continues to amaze me with her resilient spirit and ability to overcome challenges.

I had happily given her my very best, but this mama was tired, exhausted, and needed to fly the coop. And praise the Lord—my husband clearly saw my eyeballs rolling around in my head and suggested that I get out. So, I went. When my little girl waved and knocked on the front window, begging me not to leave, I went anyway. After walking and shopping and catching up with a friend, I returned to the same little chipmunk-faced girl, who greeted me with hugs and a card thanking me for taking care of her during her surgeries. This mama's heart was suddenly full and ready to tackle the meds, mouth rinse, and special sleeping arrangements all over again.

Alert: Care for Yourself!

When I am in an intense season, I can end up focusing only on my own needs, and it can be difficult for me to think about Greg's need for alone time. As we talked about in the first chapter, our hearts and bodies must be abundantly full and rejuvenated. You need to be well cared for so you can serve your husband from a place of abundance.

Sometimes when I think about Greg's need for time away from work and home to refuel, I find myself falling into resentful, bitter, and even angry thoughts. "Why does he need alone time—I need it more than he does!" You may work more hours than your husband, you may be staying at home with three little people on duty 24/7, and you may feel exhausted for a myriad of reasons. Offering your husband time to refuel and rejuvenate does not negate your own need. Recognize you *both* have a need for time to regroup, and don't let your thoughts wander into resentment toward your husband. Stress-filled times are exactly when you need to start joyfully extending grace to your husband in offering him the gift of time too.

I encourage you to pursue "fullness"! Remember, your husband desires a wife who is well cared for. Ultimately, you cannot give him what you do not have. So be creative—even if you can't escape to the mall to speed walk or to the gym to work out—do something that will push the "refill" button. Whether it is a hot bath in solitude or chatting with a girlfriend either on the phone or in person. Don't turn to thoughts of "My husband won't help me refill." Be proactive and discuss this with him, and become creative with what you need. I cannot stress this enough—the job of caring for our own hearts was given to us by the Father of the Universe. Be good stewards and take great care of yourself (remember emotionally, spiritually, intellectually, and physically)—so you can give to your husband, kids, family, and friends freely from a place of abundance.

Rest Versus Life

Greg and I have realized there is a difference between what gives each of us "rest" versus what brings us "life." What is your go-to when you are worn out and tired? Drink a fifth cup of coffee, run through your Facebook feed, close your eyes as you're typing at work, shove three extra pieces of chocolate in your mouth? Sadly, while these are great tries, they aren't going to do the job of bringing you a powerful bolt of energy. You might get a short shot of energy, but eventually you'll be left more exhausted than before—with the guilt of having indulged in extra sugar and calories.

Besides having an intravenous line to your favorite coffee drink— what truly gives you the rest or life you need? What about your husband?

Rest is one way you can recharge when you have had to deal with one aggressive client too many or have wiped your child's nose a hundred times in the last hour. As women, we often believe that being stationary is a sign of being unproductive. I'm here to tell you resting isn't being unproductive—it is actually the exact opposite. It restores your physical body, your mind, your heart, and your spirit.

> *Come to me, all you who are weary and*
> *burdened, and I will give you rest.*
> Matthew 11:28 niv

What Brings Physical and Emotional Rest?

- Sleep gives us physical rest. We typically can use seven and a half to nine hours of sleep per night to have ultimate function. Fitness devices and cell phone apps can now tell us how much we sleep and how restless that sleep is.

- Having coffee with a girlfriend and laughing. Laughter is healthy and releases all kinds of good chemicals in our bodies.

- Catching up with your favorite show.

- Doing your Bible study.

- Sitting at a coffee shop and writing in your journal.

- Listening to Christmas music or praise and worship music.

- Getting a massage.

- Getting a pedicure and/or manicure.

- Going to the library, sitting in the quietest place you can find, and reading a book.

- In desperate times, locking yourself in the bathroom and taking three belly breaths.

- Lying down and snuggling with your toddler for five minutes.

What Gives Your Husband Rest?

What is it that rejuvenates your husband and gives him rest? It may be totally different than what you enjoy. When I asked Greg what it was that gave him rest, he said, "Staying home!" I laughed because this is the complete opposite of me. But this is the key—we both need to engage in things that give us rest. So be intentional and ask your husband what that is for him. If he doesn't know, try running these ideas past him:

- Watching a football game while eating queso dip.

- Taking a nap in the middle of the day.

- Reading his favorite suspense novel.

- Playing solitaire on his cell phone.

- Seeing a movie at the theater.

- Going out to a restaurant with me (an idea from Greg himself).

- Listening to music with noise-canceling headphones.

- Laughing with friends.

- Meditating on God's Word.

- Reading a spiritually focused book.

So, as his helpmate (who, remember, should be taking great care of herself), you can assist and help your spouse take time for himself.

Ultimately, this will always benefit you personally, because if he is truly getting rest, he should have more to offer you and your family. So be creative in encouraging him to be a man well rested.

What Gives Life?

As we learn what gives both of us rest, we must also focus on what gives both of us life. Life is something that makes our hearts feel alive, passionate, hopeful, and joyful. It's different than what gives us rest—although both are important.

An activity that brings life to you is different than something you do as an escape, avoidance technique, or just flat-out keeping yourself too busy. To find what brings you life, think about the experiences or activities that feed a deep place in your heart. It's the things that make you think, "I don't ever want this to end," and afterward, you realize how fulfilling and satisfying the experience was to your exhausted heart and body.

I have something I do that is the absolute "me" time of the day. I wish I could say I get to do it every day; realistically it happens about three times per week. I've done this for years. I get up in the morning and drink one cup of coffee while getting the kids out the door to school, but once everyone is gone, I zip downstairs to our basement, where I turn on the *Today* show. I then proceed to pull my tired body onto the treadmill with my running playlist blasting. If someone were to walk in, they might think I'm super ADHD—with the TV and music both blaring and my feet pounding the equipment, it's a raucous scene. Maybe running isn't your thing, but every time I start my day with a run, I end up having the best day. I handle stress better, I eat better all day, and I have a more joyful perspective on life. This gives me life, although there are many other things that do this for me as well. Think about these things:

- Hiking a 14er in beautiful Colorado (I've already shared my Pikes Peak stories with you).

- Shopping with a friend.

- Going somewhere (the park, bowling, on a trip) with your kids.

- Going on a vacation to a beach location.

- Singing praise and worship in your car at the top of your lungs (I'm not the only one, right?).

- Cooking an amazing meal for your family.

- Having people over for a night of dinner and games.

- Teaching on a topic you are passionate about, alone or with your husband.

- Serving on the local pregnancy center board of directors.

- Going on a mission trip.

- Writing.

- Talking to a friend who is struggling.

Traveling together has been a big eye-opener for me in how my husband and I differ. While returning from a seminar, I took advantage of the flight to write. As I typed, I could tell the woman in the window seat was reading every word. Having an audience made me uncomfortable. I wanted to type, "Please, stop reading everything I'm writing." But I kept going and tried to ignore her eyes glued to my computer screen. Eventually I put everything up and excused myself to use the restroom. When I returned, she said, "I'm so sorry, but I couldn't help reading what you were writing." I thought snarkily, "I know!" She asked me if I had ever heard of Focus on the Family. I thought she was joking. Greg, who was sitting on the other side of me, could tell by now that this lady really wanted to talk, so as any good introvert would, he put on his noise-canceling headphones. The woman continued to tell me how much she enjoyed listening to the Focus on the Family broadcast every day. She teared up as she shared about her difficult marriage of 42 years.

At that point, I saw Greg turn his music up. As an extrovert, talking to this sweet woman brought me so much life and passion for our marriage ministry. Even though I was totally and completely exhausted after a weekend of teaching, hearing the impact of Focus on the Family in her life, talking to another sister in Christ, and connecting at a deep heart level made my heart come alive. However, for Greg, this kind of conversation is exhausting. He is the exact opposite of me. He needs solitude and his music to decompress and refuel. Since Greg and I have come to an understanding about what gives us each rest and life individually, we have been able to support each other more effectively to achieve this goal. If I want to chat after an event, Greg isn't the best choice of someone to download with. He needs a day or two before he's ready to unpack the experience.

What about you? What makes your soul feel like it is bursting with life?

As we focus on being healthy wives and helpmates to our husbands, think about what gives your husband life. Have you observed something that fills him to where he is overflowing with energy and life?

What Brings Your Husband Life?

As we embrace what gives us life, it will be much easier to encourage our husbands to do so as well. What gives him life may look very different from what gives you life, but different isn't bad or wrong. Learn to allow room for both of your needs to be met.

Greg's favorite life-giving activity is something that would *never* cross my mind in a million years. After we have had a long stretch of travel or stress, Greg will say, "I want to go up to Eleven Mile and fish. Does this Friday work?" Usually, I am able to say, "Absolutely, babe! Go get refueled." But honestly in my mind I'm thinking, "I just can't believe that this does it for him!" I might not understand the attraction of waking up at 4:30 a.m. and driving approximately two and a half hours to an amazing river, only to then don waders and stand in freezing cold water and fish for hours and hours. All that to be followed by the drive back home. It sounds utterly exhausting to me—all the driving and waking up before dawn— but when Greg arrives home, his soul is at peace and his heart is full. I love that we both recognize the benefits of Greg taking a day to refill his soul with life. Not only does Greg come back refreshed, but his fishing time extends into how Greg interacts with me, the kids, and even our coworkers.

Discover and support whatever it is that gives your husband life. Think about these possibilities:

- Going on a hunting trip with a bunch of guys.

- Going up to the mountains and riding four-wheelers.

- Golfing eighteen holes.

- Heading to the gym to work out.

- Going for a run outside.

- Camping.

- Picking up a new activity.

- Focusing a few hours on a hobby.

- Going on a mission trip.

- Serving the homeless with a local ministry.

Ask your husband how you can best support him so that he can take time to discover what gives him rest and life. Explaining the difference to him may be an opportunity to share what you have learned about yourself as well!

What If My Husband Spends Too Much Time Alone?

Maybe this applies to you, maybe it doesn't. I've met many women who call themselves hunting widows, football widows, work widows, and the like. They are married to men who have immersed themselves in a million pursuits every day of the week. Some women feel flat-out alone in their marriages. If you are one of those women, you may be thinking, "Erin, really, you're encouraging my husband to have more free time? He's already gone all the time."

There is no greater feeling of isolation than feeling alone in marriage. If this is your scenario, I just want to say to you, I'm so sorry.

One psychology professor at Stanford University, Dr. Philip Zimbardo, wrote this for *Psychology Today* many years ago:

> I know of no more potent killer than isolation...no more destructive influence on physical and mental health than the isolation of you from me and us from them. Isolation has been shown to be the central agent in the development of depression, paranoia, schizophrenia, rape, suicide, and mass murder...the devil's strategy for our times is to trivialize human existence and to isolate us from one another while creating the delusion that the reasons are time pressures, work demands, or economic anxieties.[1]

Since the article was published, isolation continues to plague our culture. The enemy continues to use the strategy of isolation, separation, and leading people to believe they are alone—even in marriage. Scripture says, "A house divided against itself will fall" (Mark 3:25, paraphrase). And this is nowhere truer than in marriage.

Many women talk to me about this secret pain. Here are some things to think about if this is your experience:

1. *Seek to understand the source or cause.* Spend time praying and seeking to understand why you feel isolated. Are you carrying around an old wound that leads you to feel abandoned or unwanted? We all have these wounds, sister! They are no fun! It helps to bring these hurts into the light and seek to understand their roots. Try to evaluate, maybe even with the help of a Christian counselor, if your assessment of your situation is accurate. Ask yourself, "Am I *feeling* alone, rejected, abandoned, (or fill in the blank), or am I *really* alone?" Also think about what might be driving your spouse to be gone a lot—is it a need to be a good provider? Is he an introvert whose need for time alone has gotten out of balance? Is there a deeper issue such as ADHD causing him to have a difficult time relaxing at home? Is it a high stress season at work? Once you take some time to understand what is going on, pray about having a conversation with your husband. If it is a painful "hot topic" in your marriage, seek the support of a Christian counselor, a mentor couple, or a pastor who can help guide the conversation.

2. *Don't try to get everything from him—you also need your girlfriends.* Often, when stepping back and evaluating our expectations of our husbands, we may realize our

expectations aren't realistic. He cannot be everything to you—your stand-alone best friend, your therapist, your encourager, your entertainment, and your intellectual stimulus! It's helpful to make sure your expectations aren't over the top and you have other gals in your life who are meeting some of these needs.

3. *Don't blame or assign fault.* Much of this can lead to feelings of bitterness, anger, or resentment. Remember you get to choose what you do with your feelings. If you need to have an honest conversation about your needs or expectations, do it in a manner that is honoring and kind. Initiate this conversation at a time when emotions are not heightened by an argument or disagreement. Let your husband know you want to talk about something that is impacting you, and ask him to let you know a good time to address the situation. Spend some time praying beforehand, and maybe even journal some of your emotions to work through how to begin the conversation. Try to avoid blaming your husband or turning the blame on yourself.

4. *Model what you desire!* Seek to connect with your spouse, being interested in what is happening in his life. Ask questions about his day, his emotions, and his experiences. And then make sure that you take time to listen. Commit to making choices that lead you toward oneness and toward each other.

5. *We need couple time as well!* In chapter 10, the final chapter of this journey, we will talk about the need to have time together as a couple. Time alone is needed; however, as we continue to build a genuine friendship

within our marriage, we need to have time together to do fun things as a couple.

The Age-Old Battle

Many couples have a continuous battle around the discussion of who is more tired. For Greg and me, it took on a different flavor. We argued about who did more and deserved to be more tired! Clearly this discussion or argument (call it what you want) never led to anything helpful or beneficial in our marriage.

Some couples argue more about free time or down time. Both spouses are tired whether they have worked all day outside the home or stayed home with the kids. Look for a way to work through these debates by understanding each other's feelings, and work together as a team to determine what you each need to get rejuvenated with both rest and life each week. Remember, you are on each other's side—you are each other's teammates. Don't let the enemy divide and conquer your marriage or household.

If this is a debate that routinely occurs in your marriage, I encourage you to do what Greg and I did—we eliminated it! We no longer go down that road because we know it doesn't lead us anywhere helpful. This topic typically came up when one of us was feeling exhausted, worn out, or taken advantage of, or when free time was not balanced fairly. Look beyond the debate and get to the source. Seek to understand your spouse and work together to solve the issues so you both can get what you desire. We can best serve our spouses when we feel abundantly full and our souls feel well cared for.

Being His Helpmate

Let's wrap up with a few simple tips on how we can truly be a helpmate and encourage our husbands to recharge. Remember, be certain you are also seeking balance and discovering what brings rest and life to your own life.

1. If your husband has worked all day, whether inside or outside of the home (even if you have as well), give him some time to transition into home life. Men don't multitask as well as women, and they also compartmentalize more than we typically do. He needs a few minutes to transition from his "work hat" to his "home hat." It's a completely different set of skills.

2. Try not to over-schedule his days off work or fill his weekends with projects. Remember, he needs to have alone time, time to rest, and time to rejuvenate. Sometimes let him enjoy his day off work without having to work at home.

3. Suggest that he take time to meet up with his friends. Every now and then I will ask Greg, "Do you want to go and see a movie with a friend?" Just suggesting it, whether he takes me up on it or not, sends the message, "I know you need time away, and I want to encourage that!"

4. Give him space to pursue hobbies and interests freely. Encourage him in these areas because it's important for him to have activities outside of work. If there has been long-term tension between you and your husband around the amount of time he spends pursuing hobbies or outside interests, seek the help of a Christian counselor. Work through this challenge and address the underlying feelings involved.

5. Continue to encourage him to pursue what gives him rest and what gives him life. Just as we need to figure this out for ourselves, support him as he discovers it too!

QUESTIONS FOR REFLECTION

What gives you rest and life?

What about your husband—do you have any ideas about what gives him rest and life? How can you come alongside him and support the pursuit of these opportunities?

How have you worked through any conflict in your relationship regarding the fair division of free time? If this is an issue, what
is one thing you can do to move toward more effective teamwork
in this area?

Out of the five tips to be your husband's helpmate on page 172,
which one will you focus on in the next week? What advice would
you give a couple who is getting married about working together so
that they both have free time in their marriage?

CHALLENGE

This week, ask your husband to tell you one thing that gives him rest and one thing that gives him life. Make this happen for him over the next few weeks. Be creative in carrying this out. Have fun blessing your man!

Prayer for the Wise Wife

Lord, I come before you and ask that you help me pursue things that give me rest and life so I can be a woman who is able to give to others, especially my husband, from a place of abundance. I know your desire for me is to not be a worn-out, ragged woman—but one that is well cared for and living an abundant life. I also ask that you help me to be open to my husband's needs in this area of having alone time. Help me to be a great helpmate in assisting him to also pursue what gives him rest and life. Help me to turn to you in those times I am tempted to feel jealous or envious over his activities. If there is an issue, help me address it in a loving and kind manner—setting healthy boundaries and not holding on to resentment or bitterness. Oh Jesus, I thank you that I can turn to you amidst the everyday issues of marriage, as I know you ultimately use marriage to make me more Christlike. In your name, amen.

Prayer for Your Husband

O Jesus, I pray for my husband today, that he is able to seek out activities that will truly refuel his soul. Lord, I pray that I am able to come alongside him and support and encourage him to have a healthy balance around work life, family life, and leisure time. May my husband have clear insight and awareness about what truly rejuvenates his heart, and may this be very beneficial to him. May this also benefit our marriage and ultimately, his relationship with you. If there are issues that he has around the amount of time I'm spending pursuing leisure activities, give him the words to approach me with them. Help him not to allow bitterness or anger to build up around any issue in our marriage—but specifically this one. Bring him godly male friends that will support him in pursuing you, Lord, and encourage him in his marriage. Lord, I thank you for him and ask that you help him to know how valuable he is to you and to me. In your precious name, amen.

10

YOUR FRIENDSHIP

Happy marriages are based on a deep friendship.

JOHN GOTTMAN

After reading the last chapter, you may have begun to question if your husband needs you to be his best friend or if he needs his buddies to fill that role. Now this may surprise some of you, but not only does your hubby want you to be his friend, he actually needs your friendship.

A romantic relationship should be built from a mutual friendship; that is what will carry a couple through the ups and downs of life. Common kindness, honesty, empathy, loyalty, and trust are just a few of the qualities of a healthy friendship that are a gift in marriage. Romance is important, but the flames won't be raging without the base of friendship.

Researchers have found that those who consider their spouse or partner their best friend get about twice as much life satisfaction from marriage as those who don't.[1] When I think about the couples I know whose relationships are built upon a strong friendship, I think of Jackie and Steve. They love to be together—just the two of them—and it shows. They have three children, and I still see them out to lunch and dinner regularly—deep in conversation and often laughing. They go to the gym regularly, they take trips together, and it's apparent that they genuinely enjoy each other.

I asked Jackie what the secret to their relationship is:

> We got married when I was 20 and he was 23 years old. Steve was in the military, so we moved around a lot. We had only each other, and it caused us to depend on each other quite a bit. From the beginning we have had a mutual respect for each other. Specifically, when we first got married, my insecurities about his being unfaithful were screaming (especially when he was deployed). You see, my dad cheated on my mom and left us when I was young. I didn't know anything different, and I had a lot of big fears around this. Looking back, Steve never made me feel stupid or bad for how I felt. He was wonderful about reassuring me and was very tender with me. I believe that this is where the basis for our friendship grew stronger.
>
> After having children, it became a little more challenging for us to have time together, but we didn't let it stop us. We have always let our kids know that our marriage comes first. We have regular date nights and time alone, and we laugh a lot. Our friendship has been based on mutual respect, kindness, consideration, and a lot of talking and listening. We pursue each other when we can tell something is going on, whether it is stress or an individual challenge. I often will say to Steve, "I'm worried about you. Can you tell me what is going on?"
>
> Now that our kids are getting older, we have a blast together. We grew up together and now we are going to grow old together. Don't get me wrong, we adore our children and we miss our son who has already left for

college so much—but our marriage has always remained a priority and it will continue to be that.

This story is touching because it is what we all desire at the depth of our souls. We desire to feel deeply connected with our husbands—much like it was when we were dating. We long to know that he will always be there for us, offering us grace, forgiveness, kindness, gentleness, intimacy, and honesty. With the pace of life and many other factors, sometimes we get off track and lose the base of our relationship—our friendship.

I'm sure many of you are wondering, "How do we get back there? Back to being great friends?" I want to assure you, there is hope! But it takes intentional effort.

Friendship Matters

When dating, most couples enjoy new and exciting adventures each and every day as they are getting to know each other. The motivation is ripe to pursue each other and build a great friendship. Of course, there are many other important factors in building a healthy marriage, including romance, but after a few years (or maybe months), the passion dies down and real life sets in. Friendship with your spouse is a huge part of what will carry you through the challenges that every marriage will eventually face. Growing a stronger friendship with our spouse needs to be a high priority because it will lead to a stronger marriage.

The Early Years of Our Friendship

Greg and I shared a deep friendship before we ever dated. I became great friends with his sister, Kari, in college after she and I had both dated Greg's roommate. Our friendship gave me a great opportunity to get to know Greg without the pressure of romance. After a few years of friendship, graduating from college, and starting graduate school and our careers, a romantic relationship began to form.

We reconnected after college on a cruise. Yes, it sounds romantic...but we were the youngest people on this cruise line by about 50 years, and I was there to nanny two young girls, while Greg was traveling with his parents. (It kind of takes the "love boat" scenario out, right?)

I will never forget how much fun we had together. We enjoyed each other's company, and I sensed something was changing in my heart toward Greg. He asked me to be his exclusive girlfriend. I agreed, and we were engaged within two months.

Our friendship blossomed over the next few months. However, over the nine months we were engaged, Greg started graduate school in Denver, Colorado, while I stayed in Phoenix to work as a labor and delivery nurse. Greg returned to Phoenix the day before we got married. Upon getting married and moving to Denver, we struggled over the first year to adjust to marriage and to each other. Through it all, our friendship remained and carried us through the rough waters of those early days.

The Friendship Fade

As couples marry and settle into life, their friendship sometimes begins to fade. Many things can lead to the friendship fade. Here are a few:

Overcommitment. No matter what season you are in—whether you work full time, stay at home full time, have children or no children—overcommitment can take its toll on your friendship. In the seasons where I have been home full time, I have found myself involved in many activities outside of the house—all good things, but I continued at the same pace as I did when I worked full time. It's easy to fill a schedule regardless of what you are doing. When you introduce little people into the mix, it's easy to give them more time and attention. There are those seasons when they need a lot, but we can still make choices to keep our marriage the priority.

Exhaustion. When we are running at a record pace, utter exhaustion can set in. This will affect any relationship, but especially a marriage. When you are worn out, how do you show up in relationships? When I'm exhausted, I'm short-tempered, less grace-filled, and irritable with those I love the most—especially Greg.

Cell phone, Facebook, social media. All the things that connect us can also provide challenges to connection. And sadly, I am not one to talk. I'm horrible with checking my cell phone, email, and texts. Greg may be talking to me, and my attention will be on a text I'm sending. It is a terrible message to send my beloved. Through my actions, I am saying, "You are important, but so is this other person that I'm texting right now. And although I say you are my best friend and the biggest priority in my life, I'm choosing to divide my attention between you." Greg's response has been to refuse to communicate in those moments; he stops talking until I am done with the text.

Administrating the marriage. In marriage, it is easy to regularly slide into a pattern of discussing finances, schedules, and tasks instead of connecting from the heart. Yes, these things need to be addressed, but when it becomes all you do, eventually distance sets in. Guys will especially avoid spending time alone with their wife if all it leads to is a "business meeting" and eventually an argument. Think about when you were dating and engaged, most of the conversations revolved around getting to know more about each other. After marriage, your conversations can become dominated with talk about schedules, issues, grocery needs, or weekend to-do lists.

Lack of micro behaviors. Micro behaviors are all the little things that people do for one another when they first meet but are slowly stopped. Dr. Simon Rego named these acts "micro behaviors" because they are so small and subtle that people may not always be aware they've stopped doing them.[2] Over time, as more and more of these small actions are dropped, people start to feel a loss of connection to their partner. Often couples stop doing things like holding hands, going on spontaneous dates, or talking at depth for hours. The days of wooing each other come to an end.

All these things can have a negative impact on the friendship in a marriage. As you read through that list, do you see the loss of micro behaviors affecting your marriage? Maybe you and your spouse have fought through these temptations and have kept a great friendship brewing. In that case, way to go! I know Greg and I at times have had to step back and reevaluate how we are doing at keeping our connection alive. Maybe it's time for you to do the same.

We Don't Feel Like Friends Anymore

Of all the things women say to me, this is a biggie: "I don't feel like we are friends anymore." This confession is usually followed with heartfelt tears and grief over the distance a woman feels from her husband. If this is your scenario, you are not alone. I think that we all will go through seasons where we feel connected and our friendship with our spouse is alive and well, and there will be those seasons where we feel stressed, we are both pursuing other things (kids included), distance sets in, and we begin to feel like the Grand Canyon separates us.

Know this doesn't have to be a permanent disconnection—there is hope! You can intentionally pursue your husband to try to reconnect with him. Just remember, a relationship is made up of two people—and you can only control one of them. You can influence the environment and model connecting behaviors; however, there is no way to 100 percent determine the outcome. But with the Lord's help, sister, you can make great choices with no expectations, only the hope of deep heart reconnection.

Rebuilding the Friendship

My girlfriend Sarah has been married for 15 years and has four small children. She and Paul have worked hard and very intentionally to stay connected. She is busy with the kids and he works a high-stress job with long hours. Often their schedules don't match up. Still they continue to pursue one another and have been victorious at staying connected. Sarah says this about pursuing a friendship with Paul:

> The first thing that came to my mind was laughter. For sure, we have laughter with many opportunities to laugh with small kids around continuously. However, there is more than just laughter. There are other key components of a good friendship, such as grace and forgiveness. When you are as close to a person as you are to your spouse, you get to know all of them. It means making a conscious choice to overcome faults because hopefully they will do the same for you. This takes grace and forgiveness—as you extend it, you are setting a tone in the marriage. Over the years of pursuing careers and building a family, we have had to be very intentional to continue the pursuit of each other. There are seasons of longer hours, more shifts, and sick kids, but we continue to keep our marriage in the forefront of it all.

Let's Get Practical

As we all know, our husbands' friendships look a wee bit different from ours. We've talked about some of these differences in previous chapters and the specific differences in how they connect with their friends. An awareness of how your husband connects in friendship, and how that differs from how you connect, will give insight into how to build a stronger bond with your husband. Some differences include:

Men want to know they are "liked" more than that they are loved. As strange as that sounds, most men will tell you that they would prefer for you to enjoy them, that you like being with them, and that you want to be with them—over telling them that you love them. It's nice for them to know that you genuinely want to be their friend. They know you already married them, but they like to hear you would still choose them. Building a close friendship is further evidence to them of your love.

My daughter's best friend Shannon has been married to her husband, Chris, for just over a year, and they are expecting their first baby, a son. When they went in for an ultrasound, they learned their son has multiple medical issues and probably will not survive long after birth. Through this heartbreaking diagnosis, I have watched this couple cling to their faith in the Lord and continue to trust God with this little life Shannon is carrying. In an update on social media, Shannon wrote: "The last month has not been easy but there is no one else I'd rather go through hard times with. So thankful for this goofy man and how he continues to lead me closer to God every day. Also, a big shout out to him because his last final of his undergraduate degree is tomorrow and I couldn't be more proud!" As I read this, tears came to my eyes for two reasons: it's a heart-wrenching situation to watch someone I care about face such a difficult scenario with her first baby; but secondly, I can see what a precious friendship this couple has built. Their marriage is young, but they haven't allowed this devastating situation to pull their friendship apart. I can't imagine what this post means to Chris, as a man, to see his wife's heart for him in these words during this difficult season.

Laughter and fun can be key to building a friendship with a guy. Over and over, men and women tell me the ability to laugh together is the key they attribute to maintaining a strong friendship. Look for ways to laugh together—its sets a lighthearted tone in your relationship. Often laughter makes a man feel safe with you and connected to you. Recall funny things that have happened in your relationship over the years and retell them. Maybe even play a practical joke every now and then.

Laughter is the shortest distance between two people.
Victor Borge

What Friendship Looks Like to Men

Intimacy to a guy is built around doing things together. Women often prefer deep conversation in order to feel connected.

Men prefer shoulder-to-shoulder activities. Therefore, watch a movie or take a drive. Depending on your husband's personality, the activity doesn't even have to involve talking. This is especially true for my hubby. There are times when Greg just wants me to be with him, as his silent sidekick (which doesn't come naturally to me at all). Somehow that silence can actually make him feel more connected.

Men desire adventure in their friendships. I've told you all my stories about hiking Pikes Peak with my son and also with Greg. Men love adventure. It may look different for each of our men, but find out what it is he wants to experience, and pursue it with him. I've talked to women who have found themselves camping across the country, sky diving, driving race cars, and even living on a sailboat for a year. Make the focus of these adventures a way to connect with your man—pursue adventure together as a team.

Participate in the things he likes to do—even if they're not interesting to you. I love to bargain shop. Greg doesn't, but there are times that he will sacrifice and come along with me to my favorite store. Greg loves to watch sports; I don't, but occasionally I will join in and get interested in the game. What does your husband love to do that you can join in the fun? Does he love to work out? Go walking or jogging? Join him—even if you can't keep up with him—it will draw him toward you because you got out there, spent time with him, and tried.

Show interest in what is important to him and what he values in life. Greg collects antique sporting goods. I've learned to love the way they look all around our house and the displays he comes up with. The other day, my girlfriend Ellie walked in and said, "Why do you have clothing hanging on the wall in your office?" I laughed because that was my thought when Greg displayed them in our first apartment. "Those aren't just clothes—they are very special antique sporting goods!" Become a student of whatever it is your husband is interested in. Use it as a way to connect with your husband and show him you are interested in him.

Don't overcommit yourself. Leave time for the two of you. Give each other special time away from the children. I have struggled with this over the years! I love a fast pace in life, and I often end up overcommitted. Between the kids' activities, work, and my friend time, I often feel that I'm serving leftovers to Greg. This has never been my desire, but if I am not careful with my schedule and keeping my marriage at the top of the priority list, the connection with my spouse begins to slip. We each need to be intentional about the continual pursuit of our husbands and allow plenty of time together—regardless of what else is going on in our lives. Spending time together is key to building a friendship—shared experiences are needed. Plan special times for him (date nights and weekend getaways) and allow enough time in your schedule for spontaneity as well.

Reminisce about the early days. If you feel your friendship has faded, think back to the early days of dating your husband. What was it that you talked about, what kind of dates did you go on, and what did you enjoy about each other? Maybe even invite him to reminisce with you, look at pictures, or visit some of the places that were special to you both. One year on our anniversary, Greg and I spent the day in Denver, Colorado, where we lived our first year and a half of our marriage. We drove from one location to the next, visiting each of the places we had lived, worked, and enjoyed. It was a sweet, sweet day as we reminisced about the fun things we did—about bringing our first daughter home from the hospital and some of the challenges we overcame. By the end of the day, we both came away with a sense of how good we are together.

Put the cell phone down. When talking to couples about what they have done to keep their friendship alive, almost every one of them said they plan times to do something fun together, and they leave the cell phones either at home or put away. Eyes on a screen keep you from being present in the moment. You can't be looking at your spouse when you're staring at the phone! I have decided that Greg deserves my eyes. Seeing him is more important to me than any other person on this earth.

Start doing the micro behaviors again. Remember micro behaviors are the little things that we do in relationships. Often we stop doing them as we grow comfortable in a relationship, which negatively impacts our relationships. Think back to the things you used to do for your husband or things you used to do without a bitter sigh while doing them. Whether it was putting his clean clothes away, buying his favorite drink while you were out, dropping his dry cleaning off, or making his favorite meal, do those things again. So many couples divorce over the "little" everyday things. Make a commitment to doing the little things again—with a grateful heart.

Don't always have an agenda—stop administrating. There is a time and a place for the administrative tasks needed to run a household and family, but date night is not that time or place. Don't bring out the yearly taxes or the calendar on a dinner date with your husband. Plan separate times for fun, adventurous dates and for not-so-fun family business meetings. Keep the two intentionally separate as much as you can.

A Biblical Friendship

One of the greatest romance stories we read about in Scripture is found in Song of Songs. King Solomon and his Shulamite wife had not only an amazing, sizzling hot marriage, but they shared a deep friendship as well. The Shulamite wife confesses, "This is my beloved and this is my friend," in Song of Songs 5:16 (ESV). They spent time regularly communicating, "Let me see your countenance, let me hear your voice; for your voice is sweet, and your countenance is lovely" (Song of Songs 2:14 ESV). They constantly spent time together having fun and doing things together. They met and spent time together in the field where he kept his flock (1:7), and they met for a springtime walk, just to smell the flowers (2:10-13). They also took time away for a trip to the villages and to walk in the vineyards (7:11-12).

I've never really looked at the friendship Solomon and his wife shared. Typically, I've focused on their amazing romance. But they even had a basis for friendship, and they made choices to continue building that relationship.

Pursue Friendship

Regardless of where your friendship is with your spouse, whether you feel it's strong or you desire more, be intentional about pursuing him. Who doesn't love when someone is loving, kind, brings them their favorite snack, laughs with them, embraces their flaws and loves them anyway, or plans surprise outings? It is essential that we continue to do these things in the early days of growing together and even in the more mature years of growing older together.

As you continue to build a friendship with your husband, remember that you must be committed to being the type of friend that you desire him to be to you. As a loving wife, be committed to becoming your husband's very best friend in all areas of life. Encourage him regularly and speak life into his days. Be spontaneous and willing to set the schedule aside for his benefit. Be willing to listen to the difficulties in his life—cry with him, pray for him, and support him through the thick and thin of life. Believe the very best about him and protect him always. Tell him that he has what it takes and cheer for him from the sidelines—and sometimes jump in and race alongside him. Laugh with him; commit to leaving room for the goofy side of you both to come out. Focus on all you do well together and the many mountains you have climbed together.

I can promise you that the thing that has carried Greg and me through 25 years of marriage has been a strong friendship. Our friendship has grown and been strengthened over the years. We love being together, we love working together, and we love speaking and ministering together. I promise you it hasn't always been easy. We have had to fight through some difficult seasons in our marriage, but nothing else in life has been more worth it.

Don't pick on people, jump on their failures, criticize their faults—unless, of course, you want the same treatment. Don't condemn those who are down; that hardness can boomerang. Be easy on people; you'll find life a lot easier. Give away your life; you'll find life given back, but not merely

given back—given back with bonus and blessing. Giving,
not getting, is the way. Generosity begets generosity.
LUKE 6:37-38 MSG

My Prayer for You

As you finish this journey of learning about 10 Things a
Husband Needs from His Wife, *I pray this is just the*
beginning of your journey. As you love God with all of your
heart, may this transpire into a greater love for your groom.
May you give all that you desire to get—with no expectations.
May your expectations be from the Lord—as you wait
expectantly for him to give back bonus and blessing. Giving,
not getting, my dear friends, is the way. May the Lord fill
you and sustain you with abundance, and may Christ's love
overflow right out of you for those you love—especially your
husband. In the Lord's precious and holy name, amen.

QUESTIONS FOR REFLECTION

When thinking about the friendship you have with your husband, do you feel like it's an exceptional friendship? Rate it on a scale
of 1 to 10 (1 being not connected, 10 being the best friendship ever).
What would need to happen to move your rating closer to a 10?

Think back to the beginning of your relationship with your spouse. What types of things did you enjoy doing together? Have you stopped doing some of those things? Which would you like to add back in?

Out of the list of things you can be doing to develop a closer friendship with your husband, which one will you commit to doing regularly for the next week? Which one do you think your husband would want you to do?

CHALLENGE

Ask your husband to name one activity that he has fun doing with you. It can be either something at home or something outside the house. Then choose a date and make sure it gets scheduled on your calendar. This might be an elaborate date, or it might be something simple. Even if your husband asks for something as basic as enjoying a quiet evening at home, watching a movie together after the kids are in bed, make sure to block it off on your schedule so the time won't get given away to something else. Have fun building or rebuilding your friendship with your husband!

Prayer for the Wise Wife

O Jesus, thank you for taking me on this journey. I find it appropriate that we ended on building a friendship with our husbands. In the same way that I must continually pursue time with you, I must continue to pursue my husband in order to build a healthy relationship. Lord, I desire to have a healthy friendship in my marriage. If we have grown distant, give me wisdom and discernment on what step to take first. I turn this fully over to you to lead and guide me. Jesus, help me to be the kind of friend to him that I desire to have him be to me. Help me to completely rely on you and live in expectation of what you promise me. Jesus, bless my marriage and be with me as I continue to pursue meeting my husband's needs. In Jesus' precious and holy name, amen.

Prayer for Your Husband

O Lord, I ask that my husband pursue a deep friendship with you. I ask that you meet him and bless him with all you have to offer him. I ask that you lead my husband to notice the changes I am making in pursuing a friendship with him. May _____(spouse's name) develop a deep desire to have a connected, healthy, best-friend relationship with me. May our friendship be blessed by the mighty hand of Jesus. Amen.

CONLUSION

As I neared the end of my time writing this book, Greg asked if he could share the changes he'd witnessed in me as I wrote it. I'll be honest, I was a little concerned he would say, "You showered less, you stayed up too late, you were short with the kids, or constantly distracted!"

But he saw something else in me:

> Every time you would talk about this book in front of other couples (especially guys), the big joke became, "It must be a short, one-chapter book about sex, because that's all guys really need!" I heard that so many times that I would add, "And food...there's a chapter on food—the way to a man's heart!"
>
> But the truth is that husbands need much more than sex and food!
>
> I am amazed at how your research and behavior toward me helped me to understand deeper needs and specific ways that I feel loved.
>
> At one point, you had the men in our marriage small group talk about what they needed to feel respected. As

I sat that night writing ideas out on a 3x5 card, it really clarified some things for me personally.

I realized how important it is for me to know that you really understand how different I am than you—gender, personality, etc. The biggest difference is that I'm an introvert and you're an extrovert. I feel so respected when you limit the activity level outside our home and limit the amount of nights that we have people over. I've noticed that you've been very intentional to limit the sheer number of things we usually are involved in. You've allowed us more time to be at home with our children alone. That has been a huge gift to me and has helped me find true rest at home. I completely recognize that you've done that for me.

This has led to an obvious shift in how you see me—as your husband and as a man. I can tell you "experience" me differently. I feel like you understand me better and as a result, you've had more compassion for me. You became more accepting of me as a man—because sometimes prior I could tell you were thinking, "I just don't get you or why you are the way you are." And now, I can tell that you "get me" in so many other areas of my life.

This deeper understanding seems to have given you a more gracious attitude. You have been more intentional around encouraging me either through your words or through a short text. It's amazing how much I crave knowing that you've noticed that I'm working hard to love you, to be a great husband and father, to provide for our family. It gives me such life when you take the time to verbalize through words or a text note what you noticed that I did to show you and our family love. That's huge!

It's funny, in the beginning of doing this project, there were times that you'd say thank you or you'd send me an encouraging text, and I would think, "You're just doing this because you must have just written about this exact thing." But then I started to realize that you were really trying to be intentional in how you related to me or how you were caring for me. I can clearly see that you weren't just writing a book—you were committing to live it out as well. It's almost like a light switch was flipped and something changed with each chapter and topic you researched.

I've noticed how you have taken the time to serve me in little ways that I appreciate. For example, whenever you have gone to get coffee for you—you have brought me coffee too. You've gotten up early to cook me breakfast (and I know that you hate getting up early!). You've called before I drive home from the office to ask if there's anything that I'd like special for dinner. Please hear me, it's not that you just started doing these things, I think that I just realize how intentional you've become in the ways that you show love to me. The biggest way to my heart, however, isn't sex (crazy, huh?), it's when you say thank you and are grateful for the things I do around the house. Your words or texts warm my heart and make me smile.

Overall, it seems like you've chosen a new way of relating to me and a new way of how you "show up" in our relationship. It's very authentic and real. I'm grateful you wrote this book—for the impact it will have on other marriage relationships. However, for right now, I am basking in how it has impacted our marriage. Not that our relationship wasn't already good—but it certainly softened some rough edges!

Greg's words touched me. I knew I had changed; but I had no idea he noticed! As I have learned and grown through this process, I pray you also are impacted by the words written here. I pray your life is changed as you begin to better understand your husband and what he needs from you as his wife. I pray you recognize that you are not alone in how you feel toward your spouse—but instead of judging your husband and lashing out with criticism, you are able to meet him with graciousness and gratitude.

We have a choice in how we show up in our marriage. Think about what I said in the introduction of this book: We can look at our marriage as an opportunity to embrace or a burden to bear. You are the only one who can provide your husband what he really needs.

Greg's words indicate to me that I have begun to fully embrace my role as his wife. I'm praying you begin this journey as well, ladies! Although it was nice that Greg noticed the changes in me, that isn't why I began this journey. I wanted to live out the calling given to me by the Father of the Universe—to love God and love others as I love myself. This calling should be most evident in my relationship with my husband. Greg isn't always going to notice when I make a change or start doing something new in our relationship—but then again, it is not the reason I do it. Ladies, the reason we should embrace our roles as wives is to honor the Lord and to bring glory to Him as we show up looking to love our husbands unconditionally and wholeheartedly.

Recently, Greg and I taught at a church service following a marriage seminar. After the service, I was standing by the book table when a precious elderly woman came shuffling over to me. She introduced herself as Inez. She proudly announced that she hadn't attended the marriage seminar, because at 94 years old, she didn't think she would be getting married anytime soon. (Oh, did I mention that she had driven herself to church that morning and had done her hair and makeup?) She went on to tell me that she was married to one man for almost 65 years and that he had passed away about 9 years earlier.

Inez shared with me the scene that took place when he passed into the kingdom of heaven. She said, "He was fully aware during his last moments of life—holding his children's hands and offering them squeezes. And then he looked right at me, pursed his lips, blew me a kiss, and said, 'Inez, I love you.' He was gone in the next breath—meeting his Maker."

I stood there a little shocked and teary by hearing her story. However, she continued on to say, "Over 65 years of marriage, we had our struggles. Believe me! We had some big ones—like losing our daughter to breast cancer at 30. But looking back, I see we made a big deal about so many little issues. I wish we could do that part over." She smiled as she said, "I know Merle is up there wondering, 'Where in the world is Inez? Why hasn't she arrived yet?'"

What profound wisdom from someone who had lived out a 65-year marriage. And her simple words were life-changing for me. I've fully embraced that I don't wish to make big deals over little issues. I have a choice when they arise. Yes, sometimes they need to be addressed, but more often I am completely okay with offering Greg grace—knowing he was tired, hungry, or stressed.

As you set this book down for the last time, I pray that it stays with you—that you recall the stories, the research, the biblical examples, and the practical applications. Keep praying for yourself as a wife and for your husband in all these ten areas. Remember, a wise wife builds her house—and she doesn't tear it down.

A wise woman builds her home, but a foolish
woman tears it down with her own hands.
Proverbs 14:1 nlt

My boss recently gave me a photograph he captured on a trip to New York, a tugboat in the harbor emblazoned with the name "Miss Erin." My boss said, "I figured you and Greg could use this for a marriage analogy of some sort. A tugboat is strong—and so are you, Erin."

I am strong—strong-willed and strong-minded at times. However, when I'm turning to the Lord and asking Him how I should use my strength, I end up using it for good, not harm. This is especially true when it comes to my marriage. Strength and influence are a good thing—when used the way the Lord wants us to use them. Sometimes it's easy to use them in my humanness, and it ends up causing emotional wounds or hurting others instead of helping them.

I've never thought about being a "tugboat" in my marriage or a "tugboat" wife—however, I do want to be a woman of influence. Like a tugboat maneuvers immobile ships and barges by pushing and pulling with precision through congested harbors and narrow canals, I want to be a wife who meets all of my husband's needs and encourages him to new growth and development. Use your ability to influence, tow or push, in a gentle, compassionate, empathetic manner. This will take great strength, self-discipline, and self-control to not overpower the ship that is your marriage. Follow the Lord's guidance as He shows you where you need a "little maneuvering."

Surround Yourself with Wise Women

As you continue on this journey of meeting your husband's

needs, surround yourself with godly, wise girlfriends, mentors, and women. We can influence each other and root each other on during difficult times. Make sure you have those trustworthy women in your life from whom you can seek advice, wisdom, and prayer. Start praying today and ask the Lord to bring these women into your life. Keep your eyes open and be willing to take risks to build deep friendships and relationships. It takes time, but you will be surprised what develops when you are intentional in the pursuit of deep girlfriend relationships. We need each other, and there is nothing better than when a girlfriend cheers you on from the sidelines, screaming, "You can do this!" and "I'm here to support you!" I need these type of women in my life, and so do you!

Blessings to you, my friend! It has been such a privilege. Goodbye for now, until we meet face-to-face either here on earth or in heaven someday.

NOTES

Opportunities Await

1. Terri L. Orbuch, *5 Simple Steps to Take Your Marriage from Good to Great* (Austin, TX: River Grove Books, 2009), 84.

Chapter 1: A Healthy Wife

1. Morbidity and Mortality Weekly Report, "QuickStats: Percentage of Adults Who Often Felt Very Tired or Exhausted in the Past 3 Months, by Sex and Age Group – National Health Interview Survey, United States, 2010-2011," Centers for Disease Control and Prevention, April 12, 2013, https://www.cdc.gov/mmwr/preview/mmwrhtml/mm6214a5.htm.

Chapter 2: Your Affirmation

1. John Eldredge, "Real Men: Your Deepest Question," Ransomed Heart Ministries, accessed April 19, 2017, https://www.ransomedheart.com/story/real-men/your-deepest-question.

2. Orbuch, *5 Simple Steps,* 76.

3. Ibid., 78.

4. *Oxford English Dictionary,* s.v. "affirmation," https://en.oxforddictionaries.com/definition/affirm.

5. Ibid.

Chapter 3: Value His Differences

1. Jay Dixit, "You're Driving Me Crazy," *Psychology Today,* March 1, 2009, https://www.psychologytoday.com/articles/200903/youre-driving-me-crazy.

2. John M. Digman, "Personality Structure: Emergence of the Five-Factor Model," *Annual Review of Psychology* 41, no. 1 (February 1990): 417-40, doi: 10.1146/annurev.ps.41.020190.002221.

3. "Brain Connectivity Study Reveals Striking Differences Between Men and Women," Penn Medicine News, December 2, 2013, https://www.pennmedicine.org/news/news-releases/2013/december/brain-connectivity-study-revea.

Chapter 4: Physical Intimacy and Touch

1. John and Staci Eldredge, *Love and War* (Colorado Springs: Waterbrook, 2009), 175.

2. Elisabeth Lloyd, *The Case of the Female Orgasm* (Cambridge, MA: Harvard University Press, 2005), 96.

3. Claire Carter, "Sex Is the Secret to Looking Younger, Claims Researcher," *The Telegraph*, July 5, 2013, http://www.telegraph.co.uk/lifestyle/10161279/Sex-is-the-secret-to-looking-younger-claims-researcher.html.

4. Dick Olejniczak, "Brain Activity in Sex Addiction Mirrors That of Drug Addiction," http://www.cam.ac.uk/research/news/brain-activity-in-sex-addiction-mirrors-that-of-drug-addiction.

5. Juli Slattery, *No More Headaches: Enjoying Sex and Intimacy in Marriage* (Carol Stream, IL: Tyndale House, 2011), 102.

6. Sonja Lyubomirsky, "Why the Passion Goes Out of Relationships," *Psychology Today*, December 19, 2012, https://www.psychologytoday.com/blog/how-happiness/201212/why-the-passion-goes-out-relationships.

Chapter 5: The Benefit of the Doubt

1. Shaunti Feldhahn, *For Women Only* (Sisters, OR: Multnomah, 2013), 51.

2. "Nasal Spray Makes Men More Sensitive, Study Claims," Live Science, April 30, 2010, http://www.livescience.com/6390-nasal-spray-men-sensitive-study-claims.html.

Chapter 6: Respect for His Leadership Role

1. Gary Thomas, *Sacred Pathways* (Grand Rapids, MI: Zondervan, 2000), 16.

2. Sarah Bessey, *Jesus Feminist* (New York: Howard Books, 2013), 82–83.

3. Lisa Bevere, *Lioness Arising* (Colorado Springs: Waterbrook Press, 2010), 94.

Chapter 7: Gratitude

1. Amie Gordon et al., "To Have and to Hold: Gratitude Promotes Relationship Maintenance in Intimate Bonds," *Journal of Personality and Social Psychology* 103, no. 2 (August 2012), 257–74, doi: 10.1037/a0028723.

2. Molly Berg, "The Power of Thank You: UGA Research Links Gratitude to Positive Marital Outcomes," *UGA Today*, October 21, 2015, http://news.uga.edu/releases/article/research-links-gratitude-positive-marital-outcomes-1015.

Chapter 8: Your Influence

1. John M. Gottman, PhD, and Nan Silver, *The Seven Principles for Making Marriage Work* (New York: Crown Publishing, 1999), 116.

2. Janice Shaw Crouse, *Marriage Matters: Perspectives on the Private and Public Importance of Marriage* (Piscataway, NJ: Transaction Publishers, 2012), 126.

3. Ibid.

4. Ibid., 127.

5. Kaye Wellings et al., "Sexual Behavior in Context: A Global Perspective," *The Lancet*, November 1, 2006, doi: 10.1016/S0140-6736(06)69479-8.

6. Stacey L. Tannenbaum et al., "Marital Status and Its Effect on Lung Cancer Survival," *Springer Plus* 2 (October 3, 2013): 504, doi: 10.1186/2193-1801-2-504.

7. Julianne Holt-Lunstad et al., "Social Relationships and Mortality Risk: A Meta-analytic Review," *PLoS Med* 7, no. 7 (July 27, 2010), doi: 10.1371/journal.pmed.1000316.

8. Lindsay Hardin Freeman, *Bible Women* (Cincinnati, OH: Forward Movement, 2014), 9–11.

9. Gail Collins, *America's Women* (New York: Harper Collins, 2003), 4.

10. Ibid.

11. Ibid., 3.

12. Mary Kassian, *Girls Gone Wise in a World Gone Wild* (Chicago: Moody Publishers, 2010), 235.

13. Marianne J. Legato, MD, "How to Talk to a Man," *Prevention*, December 2, 2011, http://www .prevention.com/sex/marriage/how-talk-man.

Chapter 9: Time to Rejuvenate

1. Philip Zimbardo, "The Age of Indifference," *Psychology Today*, August 1980, 71—76.

Chapter 10: Your Friendship

1. John F. Helliwell and Shawn Grover, "How's Life at Home? New Evidence on Marriage and the Set Point for Happiness," *National Bureau of Economic Research*, Working Paper No. 20794, December 2014, doi: 10.3386/w20794.

2. Laura Schaefer, "10 Things That Keep Couples in Love," Match.com, accessed April 20, 2017, http://www.match.com/magazine/article/13336/10-Things-That-Keep-Couples-In-Love.

ACKNOWLEDGMENTS

This book could not have been completed without the help of many people who I love dearly.

First and foremost, thank you to my dear husband, Greg, for being my cheerleader and encourager. Thank you for always being available to me to think things through—or maybe more accurately, talk things through. I wouldn't be writing or speaking if it hadn't been for you calling it out of me. Your mentoring and love are priceless!

Thank you to my children, Taylor, Murphy, Garrison, and Annie. You have been such an inspiration and encouragement to me. I am constantly in awe of each of you! You are each uniquely gifted, and I love watching you embrace life fully and overcome any challenge that is in your path. I am in constant awe that God chose me to be your mom! Thank you for always giving me grace when I'm exhausted from staying up late writing. Caleb (my new son-in-law), I am beyond grateful to have had you join our crazy family this year! You are an amazing person and every time we are with you, we love you more and more. Your perseverance in school and your pursuit of people have forever impacted me.

Thank you to my literary agent, Blythe Daniel, for connecting me with Harvest House and seeing the potential for this book. Thank you for always cheering me on, listening to me, and being such a safe place for me. You are an inspiration to me with all you do as a professional and as a wife and mom.

Thank you to my fabulous editor, Kathleen Kerr. Truly, you have made this process wonderful! Thank you for being such an amazing encourager and source of wisdom. You have given me confidence and validation in my ability to communicate in written form.

Thank you for working with me, chapter by chapter, and offering your feedback and direction in such a kind and life-giving manner.

Thank you to the rest of the team at Harvest House who have assisted with copyediting, internal design and layout, cover design, marketing, and all the numerous details that are required to bring a book to press. Without you, this book would not have been possible.